Communication

Effective Methods For Deescalating Conflict And
Enhancing Relationship Communication

(How To Better Your Communication Skills)

Fredrick Brady

TABLE OF CONTENT

Chapter 1: Qualities Of A Superior Team Leader 1

Chapter 2: How To Read People And Establish Connections With Various Personality Types 11

Chapter 3: The Influence Of Self-Esteem 30

Chapter 4: How Communications Function 37

Chapter 5: Communicating Nonverbally 55

Chapter 6: Have Integrity 71

Chapter 7: Recognizing When You Have Achieved Success 77

Chapter 8: How Does Power Influence Negotiations? 83

Chapter 9: Knowledge Is A Strength 104

Chapter 10: The Use Of Reflective Listening 117

Chapter 11: Hearing Your Children Out 122

Chapter 12: Addressing Your Child's Emotions And Needs 131

Chapter 13: Social Talking 135

Chapter 14: Don't Only Discuss Yourself 163

Chapter 15: Communication Dissection Dilemma 172

Forging A Way Forward 193

Conclusion 196

Chapter 1: Qualities Of A Superior Team Leader

To be able to resolve conflicts within your team, you must possess strong management skills. This includes being able to communicate with all team members, regardless of their personality types, conflict resolution strategies, or seniority.

Effectively managing your team during a tense period can help team members respect and value your input, and improve team cohesion and collaboration. There are five characteristics that will help you become a more effective team leader and assist your team in achieving their common objectives.

Communication

It is essential that you are able to communicate with candor and candor and allow the team to make suggestions. The manner in which you communicate with your team will help them develop confidence in you and the project they must complete.

Being an effective leader requires listening to your team and ensuring that your team's thoughts and experiences are taken into account, resulting in a happier team. This can be accomplished by taking the time to converse with each team member and ensuring that their emotional well-being is taken care of, as well as by providing the team with regular feedback and soliciting feedback from them.

Providing your team with multiple modes of communication, including email, messaging platforms, and digital interactive devices

prohibiting all forms of rumor

Integrate the values and objectives of the organization into the team's initiatives.

ensuring that you follow up on meeting-related actions, whether they were assigned to members or to yourself.

When you communicate effectively with your team, you help them gain confidence in you, in each other, and in themselves.

Considering the Future

When you have a clear vision of your destination, you can confidently steer your team in the right direction. You have a distinct understanding of what your goals should be and how to achieve them. Having this vision and communicating it effectively can help your team see the big picture and gain a better understanding of what they are working towards.

displaying empathy

Empathy is another aid for building trust within your team, as it instills confidence when you're able to see things from their perspective. Being compassionate and understanding enables you to forge stronger connections with your team, thereby enhancing its performance.

You can be more empathetic by:

Recognize burnout; when your team is suffering from burnout, they will not perform as well as they can, with frequent absences delaying your project's objectives. They will be more agitated, necessitating that you take measures to prevent overwork.

Recognize that your team members have lives outside of the team; respecting the roles their families play in their lives will also help them develop trust in you.

Outside of the office, spend time with your team by attending their soccer games, birthday parties, or sending flowers to their ill parent. Spending time with your members will demonstrate that you value them as individuals in addition to their contributions in terms of production.

Being Responsible

It's not always simple to accept responsibility for a mistake you've made, but acknowledging your shortcomings will help the other team members recognize their own humanity and reduce the tension associated with conflict. They will also emulate your efforts to better your shortcomings, and they will continuously seek feedback to enhance their own performance. It will also encourage them to establish precise communication plans, expectations, and required actions.

Simply put, leadership by example will result in a team that follows your direction, thereby enhancing the team's performance and outcomes. Your example of accountability will foster trust, foster camaraderie, and shape the team's aspiration for excellence.

Demonstrating Gratitude

To help your team develop positive interactions and resiliency, you must express gratitude for the members' talents, dedication, and commitment. It is essential that you acknowledge the team's efforts, and demonstrating gratitude will also strengthen their sense of loyalty.

There are numerous methods to demonstrate appreciation:

Complement your team at the conclusion of each workday for the progress they made or attempted to make.

Celebrate breakthroughs, task completions, and meeting deadlines with a unique gesture.

Follow through with implementing your team's recommendations.

Ensure that your team members are aware of your appreciation for them, both publicly and privately.

When you recognize your team's value, regardless of its size, they will respond with dedication, commitment, and the realization that you care for them more than the bottom line, rewarding your appreciation with loyalty and improved performance.

Theories of Conflict Management

To be able to place a conflict into a theory for its resolution, it is necessary to identify the form of conflict and the surrounding circumstances, which will lead to two theories on conflict resolution.

Thomas-Kilman Conflict Mode Instrument

This strategy is founded on how team members manage conflict and identifies the five modes they employ for various types of disputes. In addition, it explains that conflict is dynamic and that one form of management may not function in another circumstance:

Competitive mode—it is frequently used by individuals with a higher status than the rest of the team, such as a manager, when a fast decision is required. When the decision is made in a setting that permits for a more comprehensive discussion, it is frequently met with hostility.

This mode allows for more conversation while incorporating all perspectives and taking everyone's opinions into account.

Compromising mode—permits an endeavor to find a solution that makes the vast majority of group members happy, while also requiring each member to make a sacrifice.

Accommodating mode — This mode is used when a team member allows others to have their way at the expense of his or her own preferences because the group is unable to reach a resolution.

Avoiding mode is when a member flees making difficult decisions and expects someone else to shoulder the burden.

Chapter 2: How To Read People And Establish Connections With Various Personality Types

Whether you are attempting to make friends, improve a relationship, or persuade others to do what you want, understanding how various personality types operate and how to communicate with them will be of tremendous assistance. Understanding how various personality types function is only half of the story. Like the weather, there is no universal conversational strategy. Every conversation is slightly unique. Every individual you speak with will be unique and have their own preferences. Consequently, you must be able to read individuals and connect with them on a personal level.

The first thing to realize when conversing with others is that you are communicating with them, not just conversing. Since every individual is unique, every conversation will unfold differently. Most people don't realize it, but by paying close attention to a person, you can learn almost everything about them.

Remember that every word you speak has a specific purpose (to advance the conversation forward) and that every emotion, reaction, and movement a person makes will affect how the conversation unfolds. If you can read individuals and their patterns, you can predict what they will do and how they will react more accurately.

People have an innate tendency to think in patterns. Once you comprehend people's patterns, you can anticipate how they will react in any given circumstance. Knowing how people function is advantageous in many situations, as it enables us to comprehend what motivates them and why we should act in a particular manner. If someone desires something from you and it is not in your best interest to give it to them, they will develop a particular thought pattern. Knowing these patterns can help you avoid unfavorable situations for yourself and others.

You will be far more successful in life, business, relationships, and even social settings such as parties and networking events if you can read people and communicate with them. It will elevate your communication skills to a new level and boost your confidence in any circumstance. If you understand how people think, you can use your personality and skills to surmount difficult situations. There are various personality varieties, but they all adhere to the same models. People use the same thought patterns repeatedly and are confident that they are correct. But the reality is that this is rarely the case. They adhere to methods that have proven successful in similar circumstances and frequently fail to recognize other options that may be more effective.

If you want to be more charming, for instance, you will soon realize that being overly serious will not help you at all. You must connect with people, be at ease in their presence, and make them feel safe enough to open up to you without feeling threatened (something that many more serious people fail to do). People will not like you very much if you take yourself too seriously and attempt to come across as an authority figure or a superior individual. Alternatively, if you want to be more charming and approachable, you must appear friendly, open-minded, and understanding. You must make others feel at ease around you, perhaps even a little vulnerable, because this will encourage them to open up to you.

These "moves" are effective in nearly all situations where people must communicate. People who are more severe and formal often find it difficult to make acquaintances with those who are different from them. In the relationship, they will attempt to be friendly and expect the other person to adopt their point of view. The issue is that individuals have difficulty doing this, so they are frequently left alone. If you are able to understand how personality types function, you will be able to communicate with others and form connections that benefit everyone.

People Problems

Personality types tend to clash due to the fact that we all seek various outcomes from each situation. Many individuals desire to blend in and be popular. However, they tend to get along better with individuals who are similar to them as opposed to those who are dissimilar. This can cause a great deal of problems for those in their group, particularly if the individual receives negative attention from those outside their group.

If your objective is to develop relationships with groups of adults and adolescents, it is important to determine how much you will clash with different personality types. Those with more severe personalities, for instance, frequently engage in conflict with those whose personalities are more laid-back and amusing. These differences will result in conflict because neither party is willing to alter their position. For instance, if you are a more serious person attempting to form friendships with extroverted and gregarious individuals, you will frequently feel alienated. These individuals enjoy partying, socializing, and having a nice time. On the other hand, you could be seeking something more serious and significant. You want to discover someone with whom you can have in-depth conversations and connect on a deeper level.

The other individual may agree with you but be unhappy on the inside because they do not share your perspective. The best thing you can do is to attempt to comprehend how differently they perceive things than you do, so they will react differently. This implies that you must act in a manner consistent with how they perceive things so that they are as comfortable as possible with you.

When others fail to behave as expected, more serious individuals react negatively. This may occur when there is a disagreement between two groups of people or between two individuals. For instance, if you are a more serious person and you begin a conversation with someone who enjoys having fun, they may not consider you as seriously as you would like. This can make you feel isolated or as if the other individual does not care about your concerns. This can also manifest as irritability and unpredictability.

It would be ideal if you built a connection with the other person by connecting on their level, which is often difficult for more serious individuals who cannot let go of their need for everything to make reason. In this case, you must cease acting gravely around them and begin to behave as they would expect someone who does not take things too seriously to behave. However, if you can recognize the differences in how people think, you will be able to communicate with them on a deeper level, establish a rapport, and have much more fun in your conversations.

This is an example of how individuals may behave differently depending on their company. Regardless of whether we concur or disagree with another person's viewpoint, it is always essential to recognize their position. By understanding this fundamental truth about human nature and how personalities function, you will be able to establish stronger relationships with others so that everyone feels at ease in their presence.

There are methods to improve your conversational skills and make the other person feel at ease:

1) Always be optimistic, even when condemning

When someone is criticized, they often become combative. They will not wish to hear what you have to say and will be unhappy. Rather than explicitly attacking, try being positive and avoiding criticism. Explain how you would like something to be done or propose how you believe it should be done if someone isn't performing a task correctly or in the proper manner. By doing so, the person you are speaking with will be less likely to feel defensive and more likely to modify their behavior to be more in line with your preferences.

2) Establish trust with everyone you communicate with Trust is a crucial aspect of communication. People are unique; therefore, the manner in which you establish trust with one person will

differ from that of the person next to you. When conversing with someone, seek common ground or something you share in common. For instance, if you are attempting to convince your partner to move into a new apartment, you could question them about a time when they had to relocate and what made it difficult for them (common ground). People feel more at ease when they can make connections between their past and current events. Building trust with others allows you to simultaneously attain more of your goals and theirs.

3) Spend time listening to others

This one is a bit more difficult. Ask the person what is on their mind if you are attempting to converse with them but they are not responding or if they are conversing about something unrelated to you. Listen and concentrate! This can be challenging because many people dislike being interrupted when they are speaking. But by inquiring about their thoughts, you will learn a great deal about them and be able to communicate with them more effectively.

4) Use fundamental values/interests as a guide

When you grasp a person's identity and interests, it is easier to comprehend their personality type and way of thinking. When you understand this, you can use it to better articulate yourself and establish rapport with them. For instance, if someone knows you are an artist, they are more likely to heed to your advice and share your views. If you are conversing with someone who shares your interests, you should attempt to relate their interests to something essential in your life right now. When you connect people's fundamental values to what's essential in your life, you make them feel more engaged and interested in what's going on around them.

5) Employ advantageous body language

Keep a record of all activities with friends, family, and cherished ones. Observe how they sit, stand, and move, and utilize this information. Usually, people do not notice when you do something subtly different (such as not resting on their desk as much), but over time, this subtle difference will become more noticeable. People have practiced seating and standing in particular ways for years in preparation for the current circumstances. However, what is essential to them may not be of great importance to you and vice versa.

6) Recognize the need for status

People desire to feel significant. Understanding this makes it simpler to communicate with and engage others. For instance, group members (such as team members, club members, and family members) will want to feel indispensable. They will want others to believe that they are "in the know" and aware of group happenings. People who struggle socially and in life frequently overcompensate by attempting to influence others or gain status by creating the illusion that they know more than they actually do. By comprehending how groups (whether familial or social) function, it is easier to determine whether a person is genuinely significant.

7) Do not let problems bother you

Many individuals take matters personally. They will see what you say (even if you comprehend it is not a personal attack), and immediately begin to consider whether the topic you are discussing is beneficial or detrimental to them. This can be extremely frustrating for those who wish to communicate with others but are unable to do so. If individuals make negative comments about something that does not affect them, you should attempt to comprehend why they are saying it. You must be able to determine the cause of their behavior; this will facilitate your ability to interact with others and strengthen your relationships.

Why People React Dissimilarly To One Another

To communicate more effectively with others, it is necessary to comprehend their personalities. How one person perceives the world differs from how another perceives it. This is due to how individuals think; these differences influence their emotions. By comprehending how people think, you can connect with them on a deeper level and improve your relationships. When you do so, you will have a greater understanding of people and be able to avoid the mistakes that most people make. You will also be able to communicate with others and express yourself more effectively. By comprehending the personalities of others, you can communicate with others more effectively and strengthen your relationships.

Sociability is encoded into the human genome. We all have engrained patterns that allow us to function in specific ways in a given environment. However, it is not always simple to comprehend how people reason or what motivates them when they make decisions or engage in activities with which they disagree. By understanding these patterns, we can begin to comprehend people and demonstrate that our opinions matter. When we put the needs of others before our own, our relationships become significantly more effective. We can also begin to interpret the body language of others and better comprehend their motivations. Observing people's actions and actively listening to what they have to say will allow you to connect with them and have a far more effective conversation.

Recognize that every individual is unique and has a unique perspective on the world. Knowing how people feel is essential to comprehending others, but it is not a skill that should be developed or mastered with excessive effort. Therefore, take a moment to determine your personality type and form relationships with individuals who share it. The benefits are enormous. Follow these guidelines on connecting with others, and regardless of your personality type, you will be able to communicate more effectively in any situation.

Chapter 3: The Influence Of Self-Esteem

Confidence is a crucial component of effective public speaking. Confidence can help individuals engage an audience, effectively communicate their message, and manage challenging questions and situations.

Here are several ways in which assurance can influence public speaking:

Engaging the audience: Confidence can assist individuals in establishing a rapport with the audience and maintaining their interest.

Confidence can assist individuals in delivering their message in a distinct and persuasive manner.

Handling difficult questions and situations: Confidence can assist individuals in navigating difficult questions and situations with poise and composure.

Confidence can help individuals manage and surmount stage fright, enabling them to deliver a successful public speaking performance.

There are numerous methods to improve public speaking confidence. Some strategies include comprehensive preparation, rehearsal, the use of relaxation techniques, and seeking assistance from friends, family, or a public speaking coach.

Overall, self-assurance is a crucial component of effective public speaking. Individuals can effectively engage an audience and deliver successful public speaking performances by gaining confidence through preparation and practice.

Experience and self-acceptance are significant factors in developing public speaking confidence.

As individuals acquire experience with public speaking, they are able to develop their skills and techniques and grow more confident in their abilities. Regular practice and delivery of speeches can help individuals develop confidence over time.

Accepting oneself and one's limitations can also aid in the development of public speaking confidence. Instead of focusing on perfection or attempting to be someone else, it is essential to acknowledge one's unique qualities and strengths. By accepting and embracing oneself, individuals can develop self-assurance and deliver more authentic and engaging public speeches.

Here are some strategies for gaining self-assurance through experience and acceptance of oneself:

Practice frequently: The more a person practices public speaking, the more secure and assured they will become.

Seek feedback: Receiving feedback from others, such as friends, family, or a public speaking coach, can assist individuals in identifying areas for improvement and boosting their self-confidence.

Instead of attempting to be someone else, it is essential to acknowledge one's unique qualities and strengths. This can assist individuals in delivering more authentic and engaging public speeches.

Accept imperfections: It is normal to make errors and have flaws. Instead of dwelling on them, it is essential to embrace them and move on. This can aid individuals in gaining confidence and delivering more natural and genuine public speeches.

Confidence is a crucial success factor when it comes to public speaking. Confidence can aid individuals in effectively communicating their message, engaging their audience, and handling difficult queries and situations. Consequently, individuals who have confidence in their public speaking skills are more likely to have successful presentations.

Here are some ways in which assurance can contribute to public speaking success:

Confidence can assist individuals in engaging the audience: Confidence can assist individuals in establishing a rapport with the audience and maintaining their attention. This can enhance the effectiveness and appeal of the presentation.

Confidence can aid individuals in effectively communicating their message. Confidence can aid individuals in delivering their message plainly and persuasively. This can increase the audience's likelihood of comprehending and remembering the message.

Confidence can aid individuals in handling difficult questions and situations: Confidence can aid individuals in navigating difficult questions and situations with poise and composure. This can assist people in preserving their credibility and reputation.

Confidence can aid in overcoming stage fright: Confidence can help individuals manage and surmount stage fright, enabling them to give a successful public speech.

Overall, self-assurance is a crucial success factor when it comes to public speaking. Individuals can deliver successful public speaking performances and achieve their goals if they develop their confidence through preparation and practice.

Chapter 4: How Communications Function

Is conversing with someone and receiving their response the extent of communication? If that were true, the majority of conversations would be quite uninteresting. There would be no tone or vocal expression in such a conversation. It would be very difficult for the listener to accurately "read" the other person if the face and body were entirely immobile and expressionless.

You will notice that I use the word "read" rather than "hear." Communication requires more than simply receiving and speaking words. What is not being conveyed reveals the truth about what is really occurring. To discover the concealed meaning underlying the speaker's words, it is necessary to "read between the lines."

True communication includes verbal and nonverbal cues, as well as body language and other nonverbal behaviors.

Among these are the tone, intonation, volume, and tempo of one's voice, as well as his or her body language, facial expressions, and physical appearance.

Saying one thing while truly implying something else is quite possible! Effective communication skills will allow you to decipher concealed meanings and assess the actual situation.

Various considerations must be taken into account if we are to completely comprehend what another person is attempting to convey.

Ability to hear

Communication is one of the most essential life abilities we can acquire. Most of the time, we communicate in some fashion. It begins when we wake up, interact with our spouses and children, and determine what we will eat, wear, and do that day. The day consists of speaking with coworkers and clients, perusing reports and letters, and returning home to discuss the day. It consumes our entire existence.

Think about this: You spent years in school learning to read and write. After years of instruction from your parents and teachers, you learned to speak. How long did it take you to master the skill of listening?

One could argue that listening is the most important aspect of communication because it enables us to completely comprehend what is being said to us when it is performed effectively. A comprehensive comprehension leaves little space for misinterpretation. Conflict is one of the greatest barriers to effective communication.

Miscommunications can lead to conflict. We misinterpret others because we do not fully comprehend what they are attempting to convey.

Effective listening requires practice. The majority of people are extremely self-centered; although we care about others, our desires frequently take precedence over theirs. As a result, we frequently give more attention to what we are saying or what we intend to say than to what is being said to us.

Therefore, we must devote some time to enhancing our listening abilities. This is a talent that can be learned with persistence and good intentions, albeit not immediately.

In his text, there are multiple levels of listening.

Ignoring, feigning, being selective, being attentive, and displaying empathy.

Let's examine them more closely to determine what they consist of and how we personally respond to them.

- Ignoring: Ignoring is the worst form of hearing because it consists of nothing but listening. We pay no heed to the speaker and make no attempt to comprehend what they are saying. This terrible listening attitude entirely impedes communication.

- Pretending: In this situation, we appear as if we are attentive when, in reality, we are preoccupied and only paying attention with "half an ear." We respond with "uh-huh" and "okay" at the appropriate times, but we are attentively perusing a report or rearranging papers. This is an additional example of a poor listening attitude because, despite the fact that you may appear to be hearing, the person speaking to you will perceive that you are not actually paying attention.

- Selective Listening: We only pay attention to the portions of a conversation that pique our interest. Couples and pupils are especially proficient at this. When John returns from school, his mother instructs him to clean his room, complete his homework, and then watch television. Put your luggage away so you can watch television, John hears. Couples and pupils are especially proficient at this. When John returns from school, his mother instructs him to clean his room, complete his homework, and then watch television. John hears, "Stow your belongings so you can watch television."

Additionally, this is a poor listening attitude, which can be extremely aggravating.

- Attentive Listening: Many people consider attentive listening to be the highest level of hearing. Here, we're leaning forward, maintaining eye contact, nodding in accord, and demonstrating general interest in what the other person is saying by maintaining eye contact and leaning forward. This demonstrates an openness to hearing.

However, we are still unable to perceive what the other person is saying in its entirety. Humans are essentially self-centered creatures who cause the universe to revolve around themselves. We devote the majority of our efforts to what we believe and what we have to say, as it is of great importance to us.

On average, a person can speak at a rate of 125 words per minute. The brain can comprehend and absorb information four times quicker than we can speak. This implies that while someone is speaking to you, you have time to think about other things, such as what you will consume for dinner and whether you need to return any library books.

Even though we are attentively listening, are we genuinely paying attention? Or are we preparing our response as the other person speaks, aloud considering what we will say?

I understand exactly how you feel, dear... "If you think that's a big deal, wait until you hear what happened to me!" Few people engage in the final level of hearing, known as empathic listening.

What exactly does "empathetic listening" entail?

- Empathetic: When we listen with empathy, we listen with the intention of thoroughly comprehending the other person's viewpoint. When we listen with empathy, we place ourselves in the other person's shoes.

We refocus the conversation on them, demonstrating genuine concern and regard for their perspective. Listening with empathy can be a highly effective communication skill. Instead of projecting our own thoughts, feelings, and presumptions onto the other person, we focus on his or her own ideas, emotions, and motivations.

How can we prevent this from happening if our minds are as active as they appear to be and our thoughts tend to wander to the laundry or the grocery list when someone is speaking with us?

How can we assure that the discourse is our sole concentration?

One approach is to create "visual images" of what is being said.

By doing so, you can identify the issues, and if there are any areas in which you are unclear, you can identify them promptly and seek clarification. This technique focuses your attention and conveys to others that you are paying them close attention. Asking if your understanding of the situation is accurate is yet another way to demonstrate empathy. This could be accomplished by summarizing the speaker's words and reflecting on any sentiments observed.

If I understand you correctly, you want to transfer to the accounting department because you are dissatisfied and under-challenged in your current position. If you are correct, the speaker will let you know momentarily. If so, you can continue your search for a solution from that location. If you believe that you may have misunderstood the problem, you continue to explain it until you thoroughly grasp it.

Questioning Techniques

To fully comprehend another individual, we must also ask pertinent queries. We must determine the other person's genuine desires, emotions, and thoughts. People will not always "open up" immediately or completely, especially when personal concerns are involved; therefore, it may take time to obtain the necessary information to reach a mutually beneficial agreement.

It resembles peeling an onion to expose the center. Before reaching the center of anything, it is necessary to peel away a multitude of layers. Since each layer functions as a protective shell, an individual will only progressively reveal their true aspirations. The layers are peeled away layer by layer through the use of queries. This is an art form; it is the distinction between conversing with someone and interrogating them.

There are various categories of questions; the type of questions asked determines the responses received. When you ask a friend, "Did you have a wonderful day today?" it can be quite annoying. only receiving a "Yes" response. You seek information, not a terse, one-word response. In this instance, you received a one-word response because you posed a closed query that did not warrant a lengthy response. This issue in particular is too complex for a simple solution. It's probable that your companion had a very hectic and long day. What specific information are you seeking? You may commence by inquiring about a specific event that occurred that day, such as "How was the meeting with Mr. Jones?" This is significantly simpler to manage and gives the other party a starting point.

Examples of inquiry types include Open, Clarifying, Leading, and Closed.

The objective of the opening phase of the majority of meetings or consultations is to learn as much as possible about the client's preferences through the use of open-ended queries. At this stage, you should therefore listen more than communicate. With a few well-placed inquiries, you can learn a great deal without speaking much. It is time to ask open-ended questions. Open inquiries, which are rarely answered in one or two words, frequently begin with what, why, which, when, or how.

Asking open-ended questions will yield a wealth of data, which you can then analyze and use to zero in on one product or service to offer the client.

Again, this requires expertise; you may ask the client a series of open-ended queries similar to those mentioned previously. However, this can appear somewhat interrogative. merely by posing the question, "What were you thinking?" Although you are only asking one question, it will likely yield the same quantity of information. You will appear considerably more sympathetic.

Clarifying inquiries; Sometimes a client's requirements can be extremely complex, making it difficult to comprehend their precise desires. Other customers may have extremely vague notions of what they desire. Consequently, you might need to clarify something during the conversation.This is achieved by requesting clarification.

To ensure that you have fully understood what has been stated or to obtain additional information about a particular topic, a clarifying query is posed.

For instance, you state that you'd like to "If I understand you correctly, what you want is..."These types of inquiries may also be used during the introductory phases of a meeting to fill in any voids and obtain additional information on a particular subject. A client can specify how he wants air conditioning installed in each room of his residence. You may now inquire further to determine whether he desires reverse-cycle air or not.

At some point during the consultation, you will have gathered sufficient information to make a product or service recommendation to your client, and you will want to conclude the discussion. This can be achieved through the use of a leading query. A leading query "guides" the client in the desired direction—towards a commitment or solid decision.

For example: 'Agree that Reeboks don't suit as well as Nikes?'"The Virgin flight at 2.30 will get you to Adelaide sooner than the Qantas flight at 2.50," the travel expert explained. Do you not concur?Clearly, a leading question will elicit a much shorter response than an open inquiry. These queries also allow the client to make selections.

Additionally, you can use them to persuade customers to choose one of your most popular products over competing options.

The two examples presented above demonstrated businesses where consensus existed. In the initial recommendation, Nike shoes were suggested as an alternative to Reebok. In the second scenario, Virgin was portrayed more favorably than Qantas, making it the more attractive option. Obviously, the final decision rests with the customer, but both options remain available to them. However, by asking leading inquiries, you can often persuade the buyer to purchase a good-value item while simultaneously increasing your income.

Closed inquiries require only a "yes" or "no" response, or a very brief response. This type of query typically begins with "do, can, is, or are." Typically, closed questions are posed at the conclusion of a consultation, when you're wrapping up the conversation or finalizing the transaction.

For example: Was this the concept you had?"Can I immediately place the order on your behalf?""Will you be using a credit card or a check to pay?"Responses to closed-ended questions will be succinct and direct. In addition to making a commitment as a consequence of these questions, the consumer also makes a decision.

Chapter 5: Communicating Nonverbally

In addition to spoken language, we must learn to decipher nonverbal communication. Non-verbal language is the subliminal signals we emit in addition to our verbal communication. We may be undermining our own efforts by (unknowingly) appearing unreliable or insincere.

Nonverbal communication is possible through a variety of techniques. Included are the following:

Body language consisting of gestures

voice intonation and tone

tempo of discourse

Culturally distinct communications and practices

How to Manage Anxiety and Fear

Confront your fear and cease avoiding it.

If fear has the upper hand, you may cease doing the things you need to do or the activities that make you happy. You avoid it out of fear of discovering the truth for yourself. Due to the dread, anxiety develops over time, which is undesirable. To be able to manage this situation, you must take a stand and confront your concerns. You can learn to regulate it by exposing yourself to it occasionally. Try to confront whatever is bothering you, be it a dread of snakes, a breakup, your parents, or weight loss.

Knowledge of Oneself

Determine the root cause of your fear and anxiety. Keep a journal in which you can record your thoughts during stressful situations. Invest some time in discovering the causes of the journal entries you've made. Instead of avoiding these circumstances, you should make an effort to face them. Also record the activities you use to reduce your anxiety. As your understanding of what causes your anxiety and fear increases, so do your possibilities of gaining control over them.

Exercising

Home or gym-based exercise can be beneficial. It helps eliminate fear and anxiety by enhancing mental concentration and fortitude. The brain releases hormones that reduce apprehension and anxiety during exercise.

Relaxing

Using a relaxation technique to reduce anxiety and dread can be extremely beneficial. During a period of relaxation, the mind becomes tranquil and mental fortitude increases. It consists of elevating and lowering the shoulder while inhaling and exhaling deeply. Visualize yourself on vacation, perhaps lying on a beach on an island, as a means of relaxation. Yoga and meditation, when practiced, can also yield beneficial results.

Consumption of nutritious foods This can be achieved by eating an abundance of fruits and vegetables rather than fast cuisine. Reduce your consumption of sugary beverages and caffeine. It is common knowledge that consuming coffee may increase anxiety.

Reduce your consumption of alcohol.

Some individuals believe that alcohol will assist them in overcoming or coping with their problems. Widespread is the practice of imbibing when anxious. Abuse of alcohol will not only exacerbate anxiety problems, but will also increase apprehension and anxiety. Alcohol does not give you courage; programming your emotions to do so does.

Spirituality and God Belief

Using the spiritual technique, others can connect with something they sense was missing. You can endure by adhering to the teachings of your religion during stressful situations and when facing challenges.

Participating in counseling appointments

By participating in therapy sessions, one may decide to obtain professional assistance. If your dread and anxiety are out of control and you are unable to manage them on your own, therapy can help. CBT, also known as cognitive behavioral therapy, is a treatment option that can be utilized. Throughout the sessions, numerous activities are performed to assist the individual in coping.

Medication Although it is known that medications only reduce fear and anxiety, they can also be used to manage these feelings. This solution is not permanent. It provides only a temporary solution and does not address the underlying causes of dread and anxiety. A person may choose to use narcotics while searching for alternative coping mechanisms.

Assist Teams

There are others who experience fear and anxiety in the same way as you do. It can be quite advantageous to attend a gathering with these individuals. Some of these individuals have already mastered the art of fear management, so conversing with them about fear can help you learn more about its management. The committee has gathered these individuals so they can confront their challenges together. The meeting includes personal accounts, advice on overcoming anxiety and fear, and motivational words from those who have accomplished this feat. As opposed to those who are unfamiliar with your situation, hearing stories from people who are similar to you creates a beautiful feeling and a bond.

Adopt A Positive Attitude

Discover how to cultivate a positive outlook. A negative mindset promotes anxiety and dread, so think only of positive things. Engage in activities that bring you enthusiasm and increase the pleasure in your life. Watching comedies with your family, engaging in enjoyable activities with your peers, and going to the beach with your family are all enjoyable activities.

Importance of Self-Confidence Produces your finest effort when under duress

Athletes, artists, and actresses are among those whose professions necessitate a high level of confidence. Without faith, success in this industry is unlikely. Confident individuals deliver excellent performances.

Inspiring Others

Confident individuals can inspire those around them to work harder. As you set an example for your family and colleagues, they may seek your assistance. You are successful in making your workplace prosperous.

Enhances Leadership Capabilities

Leaders are expected to emanate a great deal of assurance when addressing their followers and completing their development projects. A excellent leader may inspire followers to act for the benefit of society. You can accomplish this by exuding confidence.

A person who lacks confidence in themselves is unlikely to have many followers. Self-motivation and self-assurance help you become an effective leader. They must be confident in themselves and in the social endeavors they have undertaken.

Having a Positive Attitude in Abundance

When a person has self-confidence, they may believe they can accomplish greatness and loftier goals. the courage to pursue greater brilliance and lofty objectives.

the feeling of appreciation and respect

It fosters conviction in oneself and respect for others. Your friends and colleagues recognize you in the same way due to your personality.

Being appealing

Most people appreciate conversing with confident individuals. It is more attractive than a person with inadequate self-esteem. They prefer traveling with an individual who emanates confidence. A potential companion is likely to find the partner appealing. A study was conducted on relationships in both men and women, focusing on the qualities that individuals seek in a romantic partner. Numerous participants ranked confidence as their most desired characteristic.

increases positive outlook

It enables one to reduce self-doubt and pursue predetermined objectives.

reduces levels of dread and anxiety

Since they are at ease in a variety of disciplines, a confident individual can take high-risk bets in industries with high returns.

Highly motivated and proactive.

Someone with high levels of self-confidence may be motivated to work diligently to achieve his aspirations and goals. Since they are action-oriented, they not only develop plans but also take the necessary measures to implement them.

It encourages individuals to live life on their own terms.

The level of confidence can be used to determine how others view you. People frequently favor self-assured individuals and assign them tasks because they view them as competent. A lack of confidence can prevent you from attaining your objectives or completing your task. Anxiety and fear do not blend well with success.

It demonstrates your affection for yourself and others to others.

People with low self-esteem rely on others to make them feel valued. You do not need to fill out any documentation to enjoy yourself and be happy. Self-happiness requires effortful effort. The attitude of a person toward something is more comparable to their level of confidence. When faced with adversity, you become more resilient to surmount obstacles. Your efforts will enable you to accomplish the current duties. Confidence facilitates the accomplishment of a goal.

Confidence and a Positive Attitude

It is difficult to get along with individuals who consistently have a negative attitude at work or at home. Negative personalities are generally avoided because they are disagreeable to be around. In contrast to those who lack confidence, confident individuals typically have a positive disposition. They are aware of their potential and will achieve their goals if they set out to do so. People who lack confidence do not believe in themselves and do not want to work diligently; as a result, they criticize others instead of encouraging them. They lack self-assurance. In the face of obstacles, they do not attempt to overcome them; instead, they give up, whereas self-confident individuals seek out more efficient methods to complete the task at hand.

The hallmark of maturity is self-assurance

People with high self-esteem have confidence in themselves and avoid those who make derogatory remarks about them. They are free to engage in any activity they choose, and they are resistant to discouragement. The primary indicators of puberty are adolescent expectation, a tendency toward inventive labor, and the need to develop self-confidence. Unpredictably, the adolescent displays profound responses to the rudeness and humiliation that he or she had previously endured due to passivity.

When you have a great deal of confidence, engaging in activities you enjoy is much simpler. Those who can control their self-esteem and anxiety will enjoy prosperity and success. When a person's workplace is toxic, he or she can engage in activities that reduce tension. One can easily control their fear and anxiety if they choose to employ the previously mentioned strategies.

Chapter 6: Have Integrity

After a negotiation, it is frequently difficult to discern the quality of the deal you have obtained. If we evaluated our performance without factoring in self-justification, this would be much easier to determine. Have you ever pondered, "If I had performed differently or made different decisions, would I have gotten a better deal?" It is simple to move on without evaluating our performance, the what and why, and the overall quality of the agreement. Learning something from each negotiation guarantees that you will benefit from the encounter, even if unanticipated concessions occur. This requires being honest with yourself. The following four categories provide a useful framework for evaluating and preparing for your next negotiation.

The four challenges we confront

The initial obstacle is all about you.

Negotiation is uncomfortable. It often requires silence, threats, and punishments, which many individuals find difficult to execute effectively. To perform effectively, you must accept responsibility for your actions and recognize the substantial impact your performance can have on every agreement in which you are engaged.

Negotiation is a skill that can be learned and used, but you must be self-motivated and flexible. It is not enough to be strong or prepared. It is most important to be motivated by the promise of producing value and profit through well-considered agreements. As a result, you should recognize that past success is no guarantee of future success, especially because every negotiation, like every basketball or football game, is unique.

Therefore, the first task falls to you. People negotiate, not machines or corporations. We all have biases, perspectives, beliefs, preferences, pressures, goals, and opinions, and so will the other side in your negotiations. As part of our journey, you will discover why your greatest obstacle in negotiation is yourself and how, by nature, you see the world through your own eyes rather than through the eyes of others.

To discover how others perceive the world and what their goals are when marketing and negotiating, it is essential to conduct exploratory meetings, exercise patience, and seek to work with the other party rather than presuming and imposing one's own views. To be an effective negotiator, you must be able to comprehend the dynamics of any scenario from "within" the opposing party's mind. Without this knowledge, you will remain in a state known as "being inside your own head," which is a dreadful negotiating position. If you truly want to negotiate effectively, you must first alter your mindset.

Due to the proliferation of smartphones and other electronic devices, vehicle wiring may soon become obsolete. This Bluetooth device can operate the vehicle's lights, gasoline flap, windows, and ignition. Although the electrical equipment was not unique, the software was, and ETD had begun training and marketing its benefits. Thomas Schnider, director of sales for ETD, met with the procurement staff at Brionary, a key supplier of auto components. He presented a scrupulously organized business case that justified the higher price point by demonstrating how their product could save money in other areas.

ETD acknowledged that such a modification would not be contemplated until the next generation of vehicles. Their excitement about this opportunity prevented them from entering the minds of Brionary's clients. Brionary posed the queries listed below.

"Can we purchase access to the software and program ourselves?"

We purchase the majority of our electronics from vendors in which we have a financial interest."How do we overcome this difficulty?"

3. "How long do you anticipate it will take to copy this type of software?"

Most likely, the solution will be implemented before the next generation of automobiles reaches the market.

Thomas and his team retreated to their headquarters in Cologne to reconsider their strategy. They had considered the possibility of negotiating terms in their own minds. After one month, they granted Brionary access to the software in exchange for a contract extension on their current hardware components. If they had been in Brionary's mind, who was obviously receptive to long-term co-investment, they might have adopted a different approach.

No standards govern negotiations. There are no established protocols, and there are no cans or cannots. Sometimes, negotiation is compared to a game of chess, with the exception that in most talks, you are not necessarily attempting to defeat your opponent and are not restricted to a limited number of possible movements. Although there are no absolute principles for negotiation, we can work within certain constraints. The majority of negotiators are granted bargaining authority by their supervisor, but only up to a certain point, after which conversations typically escalate. Total autonomy exposes individuals to peril and risk, which is typically inappropriate.

Chapter 7: Recognizing When You Have Achieved Success

How will you determine how well you negotiated? You won't, because the other party is unlikely to tell you how you could have performed better or how well you did relative to their other options.

Therefore, in the absence of input from those with whom we negotiate, we must rely on historical precedents (the outcome of the previous round) or absolute measures (our profit-and-loss statement) and be contrite enough to ask, What should I have done differently? Could I have made different decisions? Could I have said something different?

Could I have submitted better-considered proposals?

Could I have agreed with greater ease in the end?

This type of question tests your honesty with yourself. All of the conditions must be considered when defining a reasonable agreement. When the legitimacy of a transaction is questioned, our ego may cause us to assign responsibility to external factors. Upon completion of a transaction, you may wish to proceed on to implementation rather than reflect on your performance.

WHAT EXACTLY DO WE MEAN BY POWER?

You are only as powerful as others perceive you to be, which can be discouraging if you do not comprehend how others perceive the issue. Power can be real or perceived, and it can be subjective or objective in the sense that it exists in people's minds regardless of whether the other person is dependent on you or not. Power can shift, develop with time and environment, and be used to cultivate or abuse. It is evident that comprehension and appreciation are required.

Why is a power equilibrium so crucial?

So, what role does authority play in negotiations? Simply put, it provides options and, once comprehended, enables you to choose where on the clock face your discussion will occur.

• Maintaining power balance. If you hold the balance of power in your relationship(s), you have greater control over the agenda, the negotiation process, and the negotiation itself. Impact on the environment, manner, strategy, and possibilities. Depending on your goals and objectives, power enables you to choose whether to be competitive or cooperative.

It is possible to create the illusion of power prior to the start of a negotiation by displaying disinterest, describing your alternatives, or highlighting the opponent's lack of options. All of these are designed to manage expectations and give the impression that you are negotiating from a position of strength. Attempting to do so after conversations have begun is unnecessary and may be futile. The Completely Skilled Negotiator is aware of the need to precisely communicate the situation's facts to the parties involved in order to increase their perceived authority.

Maintaining a power equilibrium

Historiography demonstrates that those with authority will at some point attempt to utilize it. Consequently, it is essential to comprehend the power dynamic, identify the anticipated location of the discussion on the clock face, and plan accordingly. How and where you negotiate on the clock face will be directly affected by the type of relationship you have with the individuals you negotiate with.

When assessing authority, the amount of information available about each party's situation will be one of the most important factors to consider. The degree to which time and circumstances are transparent has a direct bearing on the power dynamic in your relationship and the type of negotiation that will likely ensue. That is not to say, however, that those in a weak position enter negotiations as lambs ready to be slaughtered: frequently, the more powerful party will use the situation to gain other forms of value, such as loyalty, exclusivity, or greater flexibility, as opposed to simply beating the other party into agreeing to a lower price. The location of your negotiations on the clock face will affect all of these options and the overall value potential of your negotiations. Therefore, if we are to maximize influence, we must treat it with reverence. The objective is not to triumph or defeat the opposition. They are not your competition. Its purpose is to help you maximize the effectiveness of the discussions you are preparing for.

Chapter 8: How Does Power Influence Negotiations?

1. The degree of reliance

Who relies on whom the most, or the degree of dependence between both parties, has a direct bearing on the balance of power between you and those you negotiate with. If you are not in need of a contract and are not reliant on the other party, your position of "indifference" gives you more power, provided that both parties are aware of and believe this. Your circumstances, no matter what they may be, typically dictate the need to reach an agreement.

This is referred to in economic terms as supply and demand.

• If there is an excess of supply and minimal demand, buyers with a need will have greater bargaining power.

• If a product or service is in short supply and in high demand, the seller will likely have more negotiating power.

Simply put, if something is scarce or difficult to obtain and demand is constant or high, the price will increase. When there is a lack of demand or an excess of supply, the value or price will typically decrease. This is true in the majority of market settings, but it is not always evident. This can be clarified by asking the right queries.

How is your supplier doing in general, and as a result, how important are you to them?

How many other options do they have to achieve their strategic objectives besides you?

How much more important has your agreement become now that the demand for the products has decreased?

The more demand you can generate, the more options you will have, and the stronger your negotiating position will be in nearly every circumstance.

Building BATNAs (Best Alternative to a Negotiated Agreement) is one of the most effective methods of gaining power for yourself, even if it is not always possible, because the more alternatives you have, the stronger you become.

The more precise your breakpoint will be, the more distinct your choices must be. Understanding and constructing alternatives, or BATNAs, is crucial to gaining power. No alternatives Mean no power, at least not from inside your own mind.

Based on the money supply, the money markets determine the best mortgage rates available for property purchases. These interest rates are frequently reported in the news as banks compete to lend money backed by property. Others will approach a bank or mortgage company, which will present their most recent offer, or they may simply be informed of the cost of renewing their current mortgage with no other alternatives presented. Those who actively buy around, conduct online research, and consult with numerous vendors, on the other hand, are more likely to obtain the best value. Determine which products are the best on the market. In addition to having a BATNA, having options guarantees that your research will be profitable. Not always are the advertised discounts the most advantageous. There are numerous lower-than-high-street-priced deals available in private banking for those with the appropriate connections and greater needs. Possessing a high-street BATNA makes it worthwhile to continue these discussions.

To assess the other party's options and, by extension, their power, we must investigate the veracity of the options they claim to possess objectively. In certain industries, implementing a solution could be expensive. Switching manufacturers, for example, may incur significant costs for retooling, procuring materials, and new safety inspections, not to mention the disruption, ongoing training, and relationship building that must occur. The adversary may be able to utilize its BATNA, but it may be reticent to do so.

Therefore, gaining control over supply and demand may be a highly effective tactic for enhancing your negotiating position. Therefore, it is essential to comprehend authority and how it affects your and the other side's expectations. The majority of individuals evaluate power based on intuitive, subjective insights garnered from observing the opposing side, or, more frequently, on unambiguous market facts. If you are the only provider who can satisfy a customer's demands, they will likely spend whatever it takes to obtain what they desire.

For many years, the oil industry has limited its production in terms of the number of millions of barrels of crude oil produced each week. This immediately affects the price of gasoline at the tap.

When the balance of power is significantly tipped in one party's favor and collaboration is not required during the negotiation, that side may engage in particularly contentious discussions. If there is a dependency imbalance, the negotiation may shift to the right (competitive) side of the face of the clock.

Absolute dependence in a business-to-business (B2B) context results in absolute authority, which can foster corruption and poor business. Governments have monopolies and competition laws to address extreme instances of anticompetitive market manipulation. Prior to initiating a negotiation, it is an excellent tactic to generate options or the best alternative in order to reduce dependence and increase your chances of success. Unbalanced dependency When one side is (real or imagined) more dependent on the other, they have less negotiating leverage.

As a result, the opposing party's authority is diminished. Consequently, establishing a BATNA is an essential part of the planning procedure (see Chapter 9). If you are completely reliant on one supplier or client, and they are aware of this, you will be in a position of weakness when negotiating.

In actuality, few relationships are so unbalanced or last so long. Power is frequently evaluated subjectively, which means that emotions, intuition, environment, and behavior all play a role in how a given situation is evaluated.

When facilitating negotiation planning meetings with numerous teams and clients, I have frequently posed the power question: "Who holds the balance of power in your business relationship, you or the buyer/seller?" Over 70% of the time, "the other party!" is the initial response. Why? Since the preponderance of us reside in our minds. We find it difficult to perceive, sense, or comprehend the pressures that the opposing party is under, so we concentrate on the pressures that we face, thereby diminishing our own position of power. Mind-to-mind negotiation is a treacherous undertaking. The majority of conversations have a much more balanced power structure than the majority of people will acknowledge.

Even if market power is plainly stacked against you, as a Completely Skilled Negotiator you must recognize that you can restructure the dependencies between you and the other party to alter the balance of power.

Generating Options

Extensive planning is necessary before introducing a new product to the market. Agreement on terms and obligations is of the utmost importance, and the manner in which you present your ideas can have a substantial effect on how others perceive you. Who is the most in need? Who you propose specific investment levels to could be among your options. You grant volume-dependent exclusivity, marketing, extended ranges, and term protections. Even if you have many suppliers or customers to choose from, which can lead to competitive friction, you may still possess market power. Regardless of the situation, you must have options or the most viable alternatives.

A challenge for account managers with a single client is ensuring that the client is aware of this and recognizes their importance to the account manager in front of them. You may even be a member of a team whose sole responsibility is to manage a client-familiar account.

Who therefore has the upper hand in this circumstance? How is power determined, and is it meaningful? The answer is contingent, as it always is. In most situations, however, the power dynamic is not as fixed or lopsided as the majority of people believe. Even though you cannot choose your clients, you can choose which ones to invest in, which ones to partner with, and which ones to engage more proactively with in order to strategically differentiate your company and raise awareness of alternative options.

The same dynamics apply whether you are selling insurance, electricity, engineering components, consulting services, or tomato containers.

Take the time to be proactive, weigh your options thoughtfully, and communicate them when appropriate. You will be able to effectively manage the power dynamic if you take the time to develop alternatives.

History/precedents

History and precedents also influence how people reason and justify their positions: "Last time, we agreed to a 15% discount on volumes above $3 million, so let's start with 15%." Current terminology may be used to support an anchoring perspective.

All else being identical, previous placements contribute to the formation of expectations. Numerous companies strive to eradicate "apples-to-apples" comparisons by continually innovating their products and services. To accomplish this, a number of people may choose to replace the individuals in command of the relationship, relocate historical understandings, or modify the delivered package, service offer, or product. In order to maintain a competitive market position, it's fairly common for businesses to engage in this practice.

When a new individual or team is assigned to a client account, or when a competitor is recently acquired and new personalities are introduced, the goals and motivations of the new participants may shift rapidly, resulting in a departure from the company's previous performance. Many companies actively switch customers to make it easier to disregard past transactions.

Existing connections and shared experience that have taken years to cultivate are highly valued in other contexts, such as corporate banking, and the value that these relationships provide may contribute to the collaborative manner in which the relationship is managed. Knowledge of how business was conducted in the past influences how business should be conducted in the future in each scenario.

Competition and market circumstances

Most industries in the United States and Europe were faced with unprecedented uncertainty during the 2007-2008 credit crisis.

There has been a decline in commercial property values, company valuations, projected future profits, and ultimately earnings multiples. Those with a large amount of debt became more vulnerable, and even companies with a large number of prospective orders appeared less secure. As commodity prices, the price of petroleum, and the behavior of the banking industry changed dramatically, the market's beliefs about risks were put to the test, and cash became king. As risk aversion became essential for survival, it became virtually impossible to secure long-term commitments within months. These events have put nearly every prediction assumption to the test, resulting in the renegotiation or renegotiation of numerous contracts in a completely different environment and manner than the original agreement.

The unpredictability of change influences individuals' propensity to commit and their risk tolerance. In other words, consistency and predictability facilitate long-term commitments. In our fast-paced, ever-changing world, the topic of change is crucial to every negotiation, determining what is discussed, the duration of any agreement, and which side is more susceptible to the influence of uncontrolled change.

Change affects both risk and value, but it can also have an effect on power. Your consumers' perceptions of their options will be influenced by the innovation, marketing, and strategy of your competitors. The fact that your competitors are competing increases the bargaining power of your consumers. In the electronics industry, the exclusive introduction of a new high-end, 80-inch, 3D, HD plasma television that accounts for 10 percent of retail sales in its target market would have an immediate effect on the sales of its competitors' televisions. In turn, this will have an effect on their commercial success and negotiating power with retail and wholesale consumers.

The occasion requiring the most effort

Time and context are the most powerful negotiating instruments. If you have successfully entered the other party's consciousness and understood their time constraints, your ability to exert influence will be enhanced. How you employ this will depend on your objectives, the significance of your connection, and the agreement's overall structure.

Any organization operating under time constraints, whether to make a decision, make an offer, or complete a transaction, will prioritize meeting its deadline by any means. Given that the worth or perceived value of almost everything is constantly shifting, it is your responsibility as a negotiator to perpetually evaluate and qualify the goals and interests of the other party. A party that is willing to pay more today may not be in the same position next week due to time constraints. Therefore, if you wait too long, you risk losing your authority over them as their circumstances change.

What if, however, the timing of a transaction is not optimal? The opposing party may have multiple options and may reject your ideas and suggestions. The solution is to orchestrate events in order to gain influence by manipulating time and circumstance. How even is this possible?

If time and circumstances limit your options, you can effectively exert control and negotiate from a stronger position by manipulating the sequence of events. The nature of the commodity, service, or contract

Complex construction contracts and corporate mergers are more difficult to negotiate than the purchase of a vehicle from a local dealership. Alternatively, negotiating a contract for IT services requires a distinct procedure and objective than, say, negotiating a divorce settlement. Numerous interdependencies and the nature of the intended outcomes render the majority of negotiations unique.

If you were purchasing a used car privately, you would likely negotiate a price with the seller. Two items of information would help establish the conversation's framework. First, the owner's asking price, which is essentially their starting point, and second, the type and age-appropriate market value of the automobile. Both parties are cognizant of this fact and will typically negotiate the price. The buyer may attempt to lower the seller's expectations by highlighting any necessary repairs to bring the automobile up to par. The seller may attempt to increase the perceived value of the vehicle by emphasizing its dependability and single-ownership.

Neither argument will affect the discussion unless you choose to consider them. There is no possibility of a relationship after the contract, and there are few topics to negotiate, so a difficult negotiation or deal-making negotiation (4-5 o'clock on the clock face) is likely to ensue.

Suppose you had a larger budget and decided to purchase from a local dealer. Could the worn-out tire be replaced? Is the automobile subject to taxes? Can they offer affordable financing options? The possibility of a connection beyond the current agreement and the need to address a broader agenda may result in the negotiation being conducted in a concession trading or win-win environment (7-8 o'clock on the clock face).

Imagine a similar transaction, except this time you are purchasing a brand-new automobile from a dealership. Servicing, depreciation, prospective trade-in guarantees, auto accessories, and even insurance are currently topics of conversation. At 10-11 o'clock on the clock face, total value becomes more significant, and the transaction may take place in a collaborative problem-solving or relationship-building environment.

What has changed between these three instances is the scope of issues that can be addressed and the possibility of a post-transaction relationship. The object, a vehicle, remains largely unchanged, whereas the proper method of haggling fluctuates.

There are no correct or wrong actions. As a negotiator, you are responsible for analyzing what you are endeavoring to achieve and determining which approach is most likely to cover the entire spectrum of risks and benefits.

Personal relationships

In every culture, relationships and trust play a role in the negotiation environment. If objectives other than price are to be considered, it is essential to engage in exploratory discussions to gain an understanding of each other's positions and needs. Most people prefer to do commerce with someone they already know and like. Almost always, the level of trust will affect the ambiance of openness and the position on the clock face where the discussion takes place.

Respect must be earned, and it is more likely to be earned through consistency and trustworthiness than through excessive flexibility or unqualified concessions. Even if you believe people to be unfair, inconsiderate, uncompromising, or even arrogant in their interactions, you must evaluate the balance of power rationally, soberly, and unemotionally, in my experience. Emotional responses to the position and demands of the opposing party can only benefit them. Similarly, if you are in a position of strength, rather than exacerbating the problem, use it to establish your position and secure commitments. Remember that negotiating is not about "winning" by defeating the opposing party.

Without trust, your conversations will likely appear transactional and difficult. Similarly, excessive familiarity leads to complacency, which jeopardizes the entire value and potential. The difficulty you face is striking the right balance to safeguard your interests.

Chapter 9: Knowledge Is A Strength

If you could read the other party's mind, you would be able to see the available alternatives, understand their actual cost base, time constraints, and the true repercussions of not reaching an agreement, among other things. Sadly, lucidity of this caliber is uncommon. However, you can still obtain some of this information by asking, investigating, and listening to other parties in order to perceive the conditions of the other party.

Obviously, information regarding the other person's options or circumstances is potent; therefore, you should carefully consider how much and what kind of information to share with them. Building power requires considering and acting like a lawyer, as opposed to an interrogator, by appropriately probing for insights. Consider the concerns from multiple angles. As stated previously, this does not involve interrogation.

ITS WORTH IS WHATEVER THEY CONCLUDE.

Supply and demand are a simple economic lever that is utilized everywhere, including the stock market, auction houses, the price of an airline ticket, and the current value of bitcoin. Everything depends on demand and the amount the other party is willing to pay. Obviously, this is only useful in negotiations if you comprehend the conditions of the other party: their alternatives or best alternative, their ability to pay, and their specific circumstances. Without this knowledge, you run the risk of making assumptions and negotiating from a skewed perspective. Even if there is a legitimate demand, you have little leverage if you do not comprehend its magnitude.

The value of the Liv-ex Bordeaux fine wine index fell from 360 to 240 between June 2011 and March 2015, and private collectors struggled to sell their "investments." Luke Sturgess had at rock bottom. His business was failing, and he was scarcely making ends meet on a consistent basis. His wife was approaching forty years old.

He was 60 years old, and he wanted to take her on a vacation, but he admitted that borrowing would be necessary. Luke's only valuable possession was the wine cellar he had amassed over the years. Due to the exorbitant cost of French first growths, he had avoided drinking them. "You don't drink a £2,000 bottle of wine with your barbecue," he would add.

Luke decided to sell 120 bottles of various chateaux to fund his upcoming vacation. He had never contemplated eliminating them before, so he conducted online research. There were auction houses, individual buyers, and specialty wine-buying firms present. The auction house would take weeks, there would be costs to consider, and the outcome was uncertain (although he had calculated what he believed to be the market value). Private buyers appeared to be dispersed across the country. Luke reasoned that if they were prepared to go this far, they may attempt to bargain him down.

Luke ultimately decided to contact a specialized company and invite them to his residence to evaluate his wine. The next morning, two well-spoken young wine connoisseurs arrived and immediately began a conversation with Luke about how he had discovered the wines, where they had been stored, and why he was selling such exceptional wines at a time when the market was declining. Luke was extremely forthright with them, discussing his upcoming vacation, the likelihood that he would not consume them, and his desire to see them sold for the appropriate price.

The two young males were left for two hours in the basement before being discovered. "The issue we have is that, as fantastic as the wines are, they do not have a provenance," they said. Because they were kept in your cellar, their market value is 50 percent less than if they had been stored in a bonded facility."

Luke responded, "Okay, so what is the value?"

"Well, as you are surely aware, the market has been declining for the past two years, and while your Latour 96 cases will hold up reasonably well, you have other wines that are close to expiration."

"OK, so how much?" Luke questioned. "How soon do you require payment?"

Luke repeated, "Well, as I said, by the end of the week would be ideal."

The two young men exchanged views with one another. They presented a written inventory that they had compiled in the basement, and they were seasoned con artists. "We can initiate a bank transfer immediately, but this amount will fall short of what you requested." Luke's reaction was predictable: astonishment. The offer of £60,000 was only half of what he had anticipated. "We'll let you think about it," one of them remarked. Before accepting the proposal, Luke evaluated the advantages of having the money available immediately and not having to repeat this procedure with other parties. The two young connoisseurs had grasped Luke's circumstance, were seeking to maximize their profits by reselling, and were conducting additional research. Luke could have received more at the auction, but he would have missed the 60th birthday of his wife, which was a prerequisite.

They categorized each consumer based on their location and size. They then sought out conditions that would allow them to achieve early victories (agreements) and were more likely to obtain a commitment without significant repercussions. These smaller grocery stores were located in phase one of the negotiations, which lasted less than two weeks. As discussions concluded, press releases "celebrated" the agreements.

At the time, phase two began with some of the most challenging conversations, including those with "cheap shops." The existence of precedents (early agreements from phase one) indicated that the terms were acceptable on the market. The two most problematic clients, who accounted for fifty percent of the market, were deferred until phase three. Because 50% had been agreed upon beforehand, the logistics company gained leverage. They were now in a superior position due to the establishment of market precedents. If the phase three consumers were hesitant to accept, they may offer phase one and two clients preferential time slots. The phasing of the discussions aided in reaching agreements with all consumers by generating power and momentum against the odds.

If the situation directly affects electricity, supply and demand are the two most influential factors. If something is scarce or difficult to obtain and demand is constant or high, the market price will increase. That does not necessitate an increase for you. That is contingent upon the circumstances. When there is a lack of demand or an excess of supply, the value or price will typically decrease. Again, the market rule is not always required to be adhered to. It all depends.

Power influences the methods and tactics employed, gives one party more options and, consequently, advantages over the other, but this should not be assumed. Those whose power is piled against them can still negotiate extremely advantageous deals with the right strategies.

The balance of power is not constant and is subject to abrupt shifts as time, circumstances, and supply-and-demand dynamics change. Proactive positioning may help you generate sufficient force to defend your position.

Both actual and perceived influence can be used to gain an advantage.

• The common principles of capitalism may not always apply. It depends on whose mind you inhabit.

•The more options you have, the greater your power. •If they have authority, they will use it.

To Establish A Positive And Healthy Relationship With Your Children As A Parent, It Is Essential To Communicate With Them Explicitly. Asking Open-Ended Inquiries Is One Efficient Method For Achieving This Objective. Open-Ended Inquiries Are Those That Cannot Be Answered With A Simple "Yes" Or "No," Necessitating A More In-Depth Response From The Respondent. Asking Your Child Such Questions May Facilitate Conversation And Encourage Them To Express Their Thoughts, Feelings, And Experiences.

For Example, You May Ask Your Child, "What Was The Best Part Of Your School Day?" Rather Than "Did You Have A Good Day At School?" With The Aid Of This Open-Ended Question, You Can Learn More About Your Child's Advantages And Experiences While Also Compelling Them To Discuss Their Day.

You Can Use Open-Ended Inquiries As A Strategy For Conflict Resolution And To Better Understand Your Child's

Perspective By Asking Them. Rather Than Presuming You Know What Is Making Your Child Angry, You May Ask Him Or Her, "What's Been Upsetting You Lately?" This Gives Your Child The Opportunity To Articulate Their Emotions While You Listen And Offer Support.

Asking Your Child Open-Ended Questions Can Also Help Them Develop Their Critical Thinking And Problem-Solving Skills. For Instance, If Your Child Is Struggling With A School Assignment, You May Solicit Their Input Rather Than Simply Providing The Solution. This Assists Your Child In Analyzing The Issue And Generating A Solution, Which May Help Them Become More Independent And Self-Confident.

Asking Your Children Open-Ended Inquiries May Be An Effective Method Of Communication. It Encourages Open Communication, Allows You To Understand Your Child's Perspective, And Develops Critical Thinking And

Problem-Solving Skills. As A Parent, Asking Open-Ended Queries Can Help You Strengthen Your Relationship With Your Child And Promote Effective Communication.

Chapter 10: The Use Of Reflective Listening

Components of the communication strategy known as reflective listening include attentively listening to another person, comprehending their perspective, and then contemplating on what you have heard without passing judgment. This is a potentially useful technique when communicating with children, as it encourages open and honest communication while validating their emotions and perspectives. This post will discuss the benefits of using reflective listening with children and provide real-world examples of its application.

One of the primary benefits of using reflective listening when communicating with children is that it fosters trust and strengthens the parent-child relationship. Children are more likely to feel supported and cherished by their parents if they believe their thoughts and emotions are being acknowledged and comprehended. Therefore, children who are grappling with difficult emotions or experiences may experience an increase in feelings of trust and safety.

Reflective listening has the added benefit of increasing children's self-esteem and confidence.

When children sense that their parents are keen to hear and comprehend their perspectives, they may feel more at ease expressing themselves and sharing their thoughts and feelings. This may be essential for children who are hesitant or fearful of speaking in front of others, as it fosters a supportive and comfortable environment in which they can communicate openly and freely.

Let's now investigate some real-world examples of how reflective listening can be utilized when communicating with children.

A pupil who was involved in a fight with a classmate returns home from school angry. A parent using reflective listening could respond, "Instead of rushing in with answers or attempting to fix the problem immediately, I can see that your fury over what occurred with your classmate is genuine. You appear both angry and misunderstood. Can you describe what transpired?" The parent invites the child to share additional information about the incident while recognizing the child's feelings through attentive listening.

A child who is homesick and has difficulty adapting to a new school or community. Using reflective listening, a parent could say, "I've noticed that you're having trouble fitting in at your new school and you miss your former friends. It must be difficult to be so far removed from everyone and everything you know. Could you describe your emotions and how you're adjusting to the change?" Reflective listening is a technique employed by parents to convey to their children that they comprehend and are there to assist them during this difficult transition.

Example 3: A young person is distressed when he or she feels deficient in a particular academic endeavor or hobby. Using reflective listening, a parent may respond, "You appear to be quite angry with yourself because of your math class struggles." When we feel deficient at something, especially if it is essential to us, it can be challenging. Could you elucidate on your emotions and how you're coping with this challenge?" By using reflective listening to make the child feel understood and supported, the parent is assisting the child in overcoming this challenge.

When interacting with children, reflective listening can be a highly effective method of communication. Children may experience feelings of worth, encouragement, and self-assurance when they actively listen, comprehend, and ruminate on what they have heard. This can lead to stronger, more positive connections and an overall improvement in communication.

Chapter 11: Hearing Your Children Out

It May Be Difficult At Times, But Communicating With Your Children Is Crucial. We Frequently Sense That The Other Person Is Not Listening To What We Have To Say. Listening Skills Are Necessary For Parenting Success. It Is Essential To Respect Your Child's Feelings, Perspectives, And Ideas. Be Sure To Take The Time To Sit Down And Attentively Hear What They Have To Say. Then, Be Enthusiastic And Prepared To Discuss The Findings With Them.

As Parents, We Appear To Have An Instinct To React As Opposed To Attending To Their Requirements. We Live In Such A Hectic Environment That Our Circumstances Do Not Always Permit Us To React, Only Act. We Assess The Situation Based On Our Own Feelings And Experiences.

What Distinguishes Responsive Behavior From Reactive Behavior?

When We React, We Communicate To Our Children That Their Thoughts And Emotions Are Of Little Importance. In Some Instances, We Do Not Even Know Them, So We Do Not Care. We Have The Solution And Wish To Set The Matter To Rest. I'm Done Now!

Responding Requires Taking The Time To Be Attentive To Our Children's Sensations And Emotions. We Want To Discover The Truth About The Situation And Give Them The Freedom To Express Themselves Without Fear Of What We Will Think Of Them. We Engage Them In Frank Conversation, Ask Them Questions, And Give Them The Autonomy To Devise A Solution Or Course Of Action On Their Own. Our Role Is To Listen And Offer Guidance.

As Listeners, It Is Essential That We Provide Our Children With Our Complete And Undivided Focus. Put Down The Paper We're Reading, Silence

The Phone, And Refrain From Cleaning The Kitchen While We Attend. Take A Seat Next To Your Child, Make Eye Contact, And Simply Listen. Allow Them To Express Their Discontent So They Can Move On. Request That They Reiterate Their Words To Ensure That You Comprehend Their Meaning. Let Them Know You Understand And That It Is Acceptable For Them To Feel The Way They Do At This Moment. Be Receptive, Forthright, And Receptive To Whatever They Wish To Convey.

Similar To Us, Our Children Face Difficult Circumstances. As Parents, We Can Demonstrate Our Concern For Our Children And Our Understanding Of What They Are Going Through By Actively Listening To And Participating In Their Stories.

We Have, After All, Been There Ourselves. Let Them Know That They Are Not Alone In Their Struggle.

The Significance Of Active Listening

Active Listening Is A Necessary Skill For Effective Communication With Children. It Is Attentively Attending To What The Child Has To Say, Considering Their Perspective, And Responding In A Manner That Demonstrates Empathy And Respect. When We Actively Attend To Our Children, We Can Foster An Environment In Which They Feel Heard And Valued. This Strengthens Our Relationship With Them And Aids In Establishing Trust.

When There Are Disagreements Or Arguments, Vigilant Listening Can Be Extremely Beneficial. Children Frequently Experience Strong Emotions, But They May Lack The Communication Skills To Effectively Express Them.

Active Listening Can Help Mitigate A Crisis By Making The Other Person Feel Heard And Validating His Or Her Emotions. For Instance, If A Child Is Furious Because They Feel Excluded From Their Class, We May Use Active Listening By Responding, "I Observe

That You Are Feeling Depressed And Excluded. When We Don't Feel Involved, It's Difficult." The Child May Feel Better And Be More Receptive To Finding A Solution To The Problem If He Or She Feels Understood And Supported.

Active Listening May Be Crucial In The Real World When Children Are Endeavoring To Express Their Desires Or Objectives. Children May Not Always Be Able To Effectively Communicate With Words, Making It Easy For Adults To Misunderstand Or Disregard Their Requests. To Provide A Response That Satisfies Their Requirements, We Must Actively Listen To Completely Comprehend What They Are Saying.

For Instance, If A Young Child Attempts To Convey That He Or She Is Hungry, We Can Practice Active Listening By Responding, "I Understand That You Are Hungry. Let's See What Kind Of Sustenance We Can Find." This Makes The Child Feel Understood And

Facilitates Our Ability To Provide The Necessary Assistance.

Active Listening Is A Necessary Skill For Effective Communication With Children. In Times Of Conflict Or When Children Are Endeavoring To Express Their Needs, It May Be Especially Important To Cultivate An Atmosphere In Which Children Feel Heard And Respected. By Actively Listening To Our Children, We Can Strengthen Our Bond With Them And Offer Them The Necessary Support And Understanding.

How To Practice Listening

Active Listening Is An Essential Skill When Interacting With Children, As It Not Only Fosters A Pleasurable, Open Relationship With Them, But Also Ensures That They Feel Heard And Understood.

Here Are Some Tips For Using Active Listening Techniques When Conversing With Your Children:

Focus Your Entire Attention On Put Aside All Other Thoughts And Focus Solely On What Your Child Is Saying When They Are Communicating With You. Put Away Your Phone And Turn Off The Television, Then Gaze Your Child In The Eyes.

Don't Interrupt: It Is Essential To Wait Until Your Child Has Completed Speaking Before Offering Your Thoughts Or Opinions. This Demonstrates Your Reverence For Their Perspective And Desire To Fully Comprehend What They Are Saying.

Think About The Past: After Your Child Has Finished Speaking, Provide A Concise Summary Of What They Said To Demonstrate That You Were Attentive. This Can Be Accomplished By Stating, "It Seems Like You're Feeling Disappointed Because You Didn't Get To Play With Your Friends Today."

Pose Open-Ended Inquiries: Instead Of Simply Nodding Or Reiterating "Uh-Huh," Try Asking Your Child Open-Ended Questions That Encourage Them To Elaborate On Their Ideas Or Emotions. As An Example, You May Ask, "Can You Tell Me More About What Happened At School Today?" Or, "How Did It Make You Feel To Learn That You Couldn't Visit The Park?"

Confirm Their Emotions: Even If You Disagree With How Your Child Expresses His Or Her Emotions, It Is Essential To Respect Them Nonetheless. For Instance, If Your Child Is Upset That They Didn't Receive Ice Cream For Dessert, You Might Respond, "I Can See Why You're Upset. It Is Acceptable To Occasionally Desire Sweets, But We Must Also Make Healthy Choices."

Here Is An Instance Of Vigilant Listening:

Suppose Your Child Comes Home From School And Notifies You Of A Fight With A Classmate. You Could Demonstrate Active Listening By Saying, "I'm Not

Going To Jump Right Into The Punishment Or My Opinion On The Subject."Please Clarify What Transpired. What Emotions Did The Other Student's Comments Elicit In You?" When Your Child Expresses Anger And Irritation, You May Acknowledge Their Feelings By Saying Something Like, "I Can See How You Could Be Furious And Hurt In That Situation. Never Is It Acceptable For Someone To Speak Negatively About Us."

You Can Establish A Constructive And Open Channel Of Communication With Your Children By Employing Active Listening Skills, Which Will Help To Build Trust And Strengthen Your Relationship. Adapting To These Strategies Could Take Some Time, But The Effort Will Ultimately Be Worthwhile.

Chapter 12: Addressing Your Child's Emotions And Needs

In Addition To Providing A Child With Basic Necessities Such As Food, Shelter, And Clothing, It Is Essential For Parents, Guardians, And Other Caregivers To Be Empathetic, Encouraging, And Supportive Of The Child's Emotions And Needs. This May Involve Attending To A Child's Concerns, Embracing Their Emotions, And Providing Guidance And Support. By Being Sensitive To A Child's Needs And Emotions, We Can Foster An Environment That Promotes Healthy Emotional Development And Makes Them Feel Valued And Cherished.

Active Listening Is One Technique For Responding To The Demands And Emotions Of A Child. This Involves Attentively Listening To What The Child

Is Saying, Asking Clarifying Questions, And Demonstrating Your Engagement With Nonverbal Cues Such As Nodding And Eye Contact. For Instance, If A Child Is Furious Because They Were Unable To Attend A Birthday Party, You Could Say, "I Can See You're Upset That You Couldn't Attend The Party. Could You Elucidate On Your Travel Motivations?" By Attentively Listening To The Child, You Can Demonstrate That You Are Interested In Learning About Their Thoughts And Emotions.

Recognizing A Child's Emotions Is Another Method For Responding To Their Desires And Emotions. Even If You Disagree With Or Disapprove Of The Child's Feelings, You Must Acknowledge And Validate Them. Example: "I Understand Why You're Upset Because Your Friend Stole Your Toy Without Your Permission." "I Understand Why You Are Upset With Me. It Is Unacceptable For Someone To Take Something Without Asking." By Acknowledging The Child's Emotions,

You Help Him Or Her To Feel Understood And Supported.

When A Child Is Experiencing Negative Emotions, It Is Essential To Actively Attend To Them, Acknowledge Their Feelings, And Offer Comfort And Guidance.

This Can Be Accomplished By Hugging Or Holding The Child's Hand, Speaking Soothing Words To Them, Or Providing Them With Coping Mechanisms. For Example, You Might Tell A Child Who Is Anxious About Starting A New School, "I Understand That Starting A New School Can Be Intimidating, But I Have Faith In You. You Will Succeed Magnificently! If You Begin To Feel Apprehensive, You Can Also Take A Few Deep Breaths Or Consider All The Exciting Things You'll Get To Do At School. You Are Helping The Child Feel More Secure And Capable Of Managing Their Emotions By Providing Solace And Guidance.

Effective Communication Requires Consideration Of A Child's Emotions And

Desires. By Actively Listening, Recognizing A Child's Emotions, And Providing Comfort And Guidance, We Can Create A Positive, Uplifting Environment In Which The Child Feels Cherished And Valued.

Chapter 13: Social Talking

In society, there are numerous avenues for communication. From small to large, from ordinary to significant, they are all colored. Obviously, conversing at a wedding is not the same as crying at a funeral. However, regardless of your location, you should always remember the most fundamental rule: listen and be receptive.

IN PARTIES

I find every crowded party both immensely appealing and somewhat challenging. In a noisy environment, your voice will be inaudible no matter how forcefully you speak. I have no reason to introduce myself to this person while holding a fancy glass, as I do not consume. Most of the time, I simply cross my arms comfortably across my chest. Some viewers may perceive Larry King as being too reserved, but that's okay; I'll strike up a conversation with someone. I'm not shy, and if you talk to me, you'll find that I'm quite receptive. At the celebration, you shouldn't allow yourself to be too serious or quiet. Join the group, make a brief introduction, and grin briefly in response to the current topic of conversation.

At both large and small gatherings, we typically encounter at least one or two familiar faces, such as a neighbor or colleague. You could easily begin a story with this. Consider that they are comparable to you and share your similarities; therefore, it is not difficult to generate conversation topics!

AMAZING QUESTIONS

Knowing how to pose questions is vital for effective communication. Since I am typically inquisitive, I frequently ask "Why?" at social gatherings. A friend informed me that his entire family was moving to another city. Why so? A woman who changed professions recently. Why? Someone has just entered the police station, so I will inquire about their purpose for doing so immediately.

I am likely the host of the show who poses this query the most. I believe the topic is excellent. Why? It is uncomplicated, straightforward, and effective. The question "Why?" may help you begin an evocative and engaging story.

WAYS TO VERY CLEARLY "Withdraw"

If you're bored or feel that it's time to cease talking, here's a quick way to end the conversation. Say, "I'm sorry, I need to use the restroom." Become a bit "urgent," and no one will halt you! When you return, you can initiate a new narrative with someone.

You may also shout, "Stacey, do you know Bill?" if you see a familiar visage, such as a friend named Stacey. You can choose what to say when Stacey shakes Bill's hand: "I know you two have a lot to talk about, so I'll be back in a minute!" Of course, no one will hold it against you if you abandon a party that is extremely crowded. Stacey may find it difficult to "forgive" you if Bill has a monotonous and offensive manner of speech. Therefore, it is preferable to handle this delicate issue on your own.

You may utilize the following phrases and words:

1. "I'm going to find another dish because this one is so bad."

2. Please excuse me; I'm going over there to introduce myself to the manager.

3. Oh, I haven't seen that acquaintance over there in a while; perhaps I can visit for a while.

It is vital that you do not become excessively preoccupied with withdrawal. Do not spend an excessive amount of time seeking for someone before explaining your exit. Regard your withdrawal as normal. Never, ever give the impression that you don't want to speak with someone. Simply remark, "It was a pleasure to speak with you," and your interlocutor will be pleased and you will have demonstrated sufficient courtesy. Then, leaving progressively is not disrespectful.

RETURNING TO THE WOMEN'S DISCUSSION

There will be times when you wish to rejoin the previous conversation group, as well as times when you decide to leave. In addition, I do not undervalue this skill. Even if you are not an experienced MC, you can effectively manage this situation.

These are the primary methods:

+ Select a topic that appeals to everyone.

Pose questions that encourage everyone to share their thoughts. Start with simple topics and avoid confronting difficult subjects. It is also prudent to avoid abstruse or complex topics that are best left to experts.

+ Consider the perspectives of others.

Do not dwell excessively on your viewpoint. Asking for their feedback will make you more memorable to them. Henry Kissinger, who devoted his life to the study of spoken language, took this notion very seriously. Kissinger always solicits the opinions of his counterparts, even when the topic falls within his area of expertise.

+ Encourage the timid member of the group to speak up more.

I constantly consider how to include all of my friends in the roundtable. Specifically for those who are reserved or reticent communicators. If the person to my left is very talkative and the person to my right is very quiet, it is my responsibility to find a balance of enthusiasm for both parties. I am constantly observing the cautious, reserved individuals to determine how they respond to the hotly contested topic. Use Henry Kissinger's famous question, "And you, what do you think about this?" to elicit their thoughts. The individual will eventually overcome their timidity and contribute to the conversation.

Pose questions to which they can respond. If the conversation is about education, you could ask, "Your daughter appears to be attending X High School, isn't she?" How is she currently doing in her studies?

+ Do not dominate the narrative.

The danger of public speaking is desiring to control the story. Simply summarize the main points of your extensive explanation. In addition to your own story, there are many other people's to discuss.

Overspeaking (speaking excessively) does not induce empathy in the listener. Even the positive impressions you've worked so hard to cultivate in the past are destroyed by this. Excessive speech will weary people and may result in a costly loss of credibility.

+ Refrain from addressing "professors, doctors"

In public, bear in mind that not everyone is a knowledgeable expert, so avoid bringing up topics that appear to be extremely academic or that require a detailed, scientific response from the other person. Do not dig too deeply; instead, urge the issue until it is resolved, as if you were conducting an oral examination.

Using too few words, words that are difficult to understand, and terminology that is uncommon but specialized can also have negative effects. Initially, the incapacity to comprehend causes difficulties for the listener. Second, you will develop a terrible reputation as someone who flaunts their "macro" knowledge or has the expertise to articulate it adequately! Does anyone else wish to speak with you right now?

+ The "What if...?" speculation. What if...?'

If you want to have an intriguing and lively discussion, you cannot afford to avoid this type of question.

What would happen if Bin Laden was captured?

What would you purchase immediately if you won the lottery?

There is no subject or quantity limit on hypothetical inquiries. You can always consider them in a more humorous light. We will contribute more vivid details to the plot. The responses are also vivid.

Regardless of your gender, age, or social status, choose topics that are relevant to everyone. Anyone may respond and dispute with your hypothetical inquiry. So you are effective!

When I encounter a large number of people at events, there is a topic that I often consider...

Imagine that you are the only person on an island with your closest friend, who is also dying of cancer. Before passing away, he informed his associates that no one knew he had $100,000 in the bank. He provided you with the account password and expressed his final wish to donate the funds to his son, who was preparing for the college entrance exam. He ultimately died away. But the young man had no desire to learn; he was merely a toy. If you give him that money, he will find employment in taverns and clubs immediately. Meanwhile, your son is a hard worker who is preparing to enroll in college and aspires to become a doctor. So, to whom would you give this money?

I've told this story and posed this query to a wide range of individuals, from heads of state to recently enlisted soldiers. And whoever I question, I usually initiate a "thrilling" and highly engaging discussion. Everyone has a unique perspective. However, everyone is very enthusiastic. Sometimes, this anecdote is discussed over dinner.

Under the name Mensa, a group of talented individuals from all over the globe has gathered. This group frequently enjoys bringing up engaging human existence-related debate topics, which fosters innovative thought and logical reasoning.

Here, we'll attempt to delve deeper into their two compelling stories:

1. Four men are in a mine. Unfortunately, the mine caved in. There was only one escape hole.

2. "What would you do if a god granted you invisibility?" This topic was once discussed at a Mensa group meeting I attended. One promised to become invisible through the use of magic in order to perform positive deeds for others. However, not everyone is as courteous. One stated that he would enhance his business through deception. If an invisible ghost could manipulate the stock market, it would not be for amusement; rather, it would transform a homeless man into a billionaire with the same fortune as Bill Gates. Others assert he will travel to the racetrack to steal

sensitive information and become affluent. Without a doubt, you will use this magical ability to control the entire planet. What would you do, for good or for personal gain, if you were invisible?

Finally, it could be argued that this form of hypothetical inquiry has numerous applications. Occasionally, the conversation meanders on without generating an engaging new topic. Speculative inquiries must be made in the appropriate context, at the appropriate time, and with the appropriate degree of moderation. Avoid making commonplace assumptions when conversing with a hermit, for instance. It is impolite to say to a friend's wife, "If your spouse is going out with someone tonight..." Such assumptions could have calamitous results, such as getting slapped by your wife and then having your husband beat you up. In a nutshell, I am arguing that we should not recklessly ignite a conflict weapon; only a captivating story will suffice!

+ Pay attention to your surroundings.

Party organizers with experience frequently arrange rooms and residences to create a cozy and private atmosphere. Depending on your artistic or scientific preferences, a gentle floral vase or angular decorations have a significant effect on the party's psychology. I am neither an architect nor a horticulturist, but I can tell you how the CNN "Larry King Live" filming area is organized. mine.

CNN employed professional designers to construct my chair and the chairs for visitors. From these chairs, they were able to create an environment that fosters familiarity and closeness between host and guest. Our table lacked flowers, and the wall behind it did not feature oversized photographs of New York or Washington. There are only "perspective" seats and a map affixed on the wall. I find the music to be simple but melodic. We appreciate these inventive and innovative designers!

You do not have to choose a very colorful environment for your friends to converse in. Additionally, it is not reasonable to neglect the time because of the picturesque location. Consider relocating to a home with a fan or air conditioner if, for instance, the weather is hot and muggy today and your yard is typically a wonderful place to enjoy tea and wine. Additionally, precisely position your seats. If the space is limited, request that guests sit close together; otherwise, enable them to sit outside. If there aren't enough spaces, create a buffet with flexibility. Attempting to navigate a party while crowded around a small table is the most uncomfortable situation possible.

+ Communicate with the opposite species

Since the beginning of time, people have recognized how challenging it can be to converse with companions of the opposite sex, particularly when they've just met. Even I am convinced that failure is highly probable.

In the past, a man would approach a woman at a dinner party with phrases such as "You look so gorgeous!" or "Have you met me before?

It may be difficult to initiate a polite conversation with someone of the opposite sex. Men are not the only ones who have this concern; women do as well. Women have certain taboos, which makes it even more difficult for them.

If you're a woman, you can still converse with your friends at a small gathering. However, in public, a lady must be very shrewd to avoid being criticized for "losing her charm" and approaching an attractive male (whom she has never met) to strike up a conversation.

When I was in high school, it was common for parents to forbid their daughters from calling their boyfriends.

There are no longer any taboos. Gifts for lovers are always limitless and can even soar. It is common for a girl to contact a guy first. So let's return to the main topic: how to interact well with a friend of the opposite sex.

"Nature" always gives us the self-assurance and comfort we need to communicate freely, without stuttering or embarrassment. You know, the only piece of advice Arthur Godfrey ever gave me was to "speak naturally." The problem with communicating with the woman is... Nonetheless, I needed a brief conversation with you for some purpose. I'm Larry King; pleased to meet you.

Ask Godfrey some concerns. If she responds, your conversation will be engaging. If not, you are considered "lost" because, regardless of how challenging the conversation is, it will terminate in silence if the other party does not respond.

Inversely, what will you discuss if the other party appears to share your interest?

Everyone appears to be pondering if Mike Tyson will be permitted to fight again. What is your opinion?

I recently heard that the price of gold had decreased; do you anticipate that this trend will continue?

Such questions serve two purposes: to help you get to know one another better than the brief introductions you both gave, and to allow you to "test" your opponent's knowledge in order to determine their level of education and whether or not they are interested in the news.

If a woman responds quickly to your initial inquiry, "I'm sorry, Mike Tyson isn't licensed," you can assume she is genuinely interested in the event. But if she responds, "Oh, I don't know anything about Mike Tyson, why can't he fight anymore?" you must quickly complete the story and convey your thoughts. Quickly shift to a new topic.

Similarly, if his response to the second question is, "This morning I read an article analyzing the price of gold plummeting," you are free to discuss gold prices with him.

My advice is to promptly learn as much as possible about the other person when conversing with someone of the opposite sex. Discussing topics within your area of expertise will pique their interest. And talk about it in a casual manner. If you possess wit and a sense of humor, ask her if she appreciates having fun. If you consider yourself to be serious, you should determine if he is also serious. It is essential to determine if your companion shares your passion for movies or sports if you share these interests. If the other individual appears uninterested in you or what you have to say, it is advisable to withdraw politely. There will undoubtedly be someone you can converse with in the throng.

Small-scale banquets

I find it much easier to converse over meals with small groups. I believe you both share my feelings. Because the majority of attendees already know one another, the conversation will flow more naturally and be more convenient.

Enhance the atmosphere at the supper table? Not at all tricky! Everyone is encouraged to discuss and offer opinions, so long as current events are discussed. There are occasionally unanticipated occurrences, such as a person who had a terrible day at work or is dealing with a difficult personal problem. When this occurs, you should be sensitive; avoid bringing up their personal distress and let's converse about something cozier and more engaging.

A PARTY, a wedding, a jubilee, etc.

Birthday parties and nuptials are examples of occasions where close friends can have a good time together. Whether you know someone well or not, you can converse with them in the most relaxed manner in these settings.

Are you familiar with the bride? I am her best friend. But I did not recognize the visage of the groom until just now. Her family is exemplary, and she is lovely.

New acquaintances can readily discuss the bride, the groom, and the party's activities. There are a multitude of topics that can be discussed, such as "Where will they travel for their honeymoon?

However, there will be more grief than at the funeral alone. A crucial tip to follow when communicating with the deceased's family is to choose your words cautiously. Keep your remarks minimal and appropriate. It is not necessary to express sympathy by stating, "I know you are terribly sad and heartbroken..." Insensitive condolences only exacerbate the family's anguish. Why don't you consider how upset the proprietor will be when he hears your remarks?

What should be said? Tell us about the recollections left behind by the deceased. At John's funeral, I recalled saying, "I'll never forget being with John on that Friday night as I was dying in the hospital, and then driving him home in the torrential rain.

Bring up fond memories if you are close to your family: "Do you remember how Fritz used to entertain his peers with jokes? I've never heard funnier stories than the ones he told." Perhaps you have lit a candle in the gloomy funeral setting when discussing such topics. This is an opportunity to share those priceless memories with the family, particularly with regard to information they may not already know about the deceased.

Even if you did not know the deceased very well, you can discuss their accomplishments. such as their children's prosperity, how they were once "shining pearls," etc. You should not worry excessively about what to say at a funeral. What would you like to hear if you attempted to envision yourself as a family member? The better and more direct a statement is, the better it is.

Because ultimately, in this situation, no one will care whether you are a gifted orator or a keen orator. Simply convey your sincere condolences. That's enough; she's truly gone.

The fundamentals are the same if you are selected as the spokesperson for the funeral. Please use the simplest and most straightforward language feasible. Despite my lack of expertise, I have observed the following:

In October 1993, Bob Woolf, my closest friend and colleague, passed away unexpectedly. I have maintained a close relationship with the Bob Woolf family for many years. I frequently collaborate with Bob and his intelligent daughter, Stacey Woolf. In my memory, Bob has always come across as a distinguished, talented, and humorous individual. Bob enjoys my highest regard. The news of his departure left us all in disbelief. Bob passed away peacefully in his sleep on a cool autumn afternoon in Florida, just a few days after hosting my 60th birthday party in Washington. I was one of five invited speakers at Stacey's funeral. Due to my lack of readiness, I felt both honored and embarrassed. The death of Bob still causes me to convulse. How can this unconscious consciousness determine what to say and what not to say? Am I missing something here? I instructed myself to maintain composure and speak with confidence at the time.

I am the last one to speak. The first four speakers were outstanding, especially Bob's rabbi. Now it was my turn... Possibly the most difficult speech I've ever delivered. However, it wasn't a sermon. These are the emotions and recollections I share with the Woolf family, along with everyone else who has experienced this perplexing situation.

When we said our final farewells, I was standing next to the tightly sealed casket of my dear friend. Upon noticing Stacey's and the other people's dejected expressions, I abruptly recognized that everyone in the room was experiencing the same sorrow as I. I needed to keep my emotions in check. I then began to say, "I'm Bob's second Larry; he has two closest friends named Larry. Bob did not know who to speak with when I and Larry Bird called together.

Some individuals began weeping during these opening remarks. Bob was consistently humorous and humorous throughout his life, always anxious to crack jokes. Bob enjoys taking photographs, as you may already know. Everywhere he travels, he is constantly interested in taking photographs. Bob will promptly mention the invention of the camera if you ask him to name the greatest human invention.

So, despite the tense atmosphere, we were able to relax for a brief time. I believe I am heading in the right direction. Regarding Bob, I've selected the most suitable approach. I believe that you should obey your intuition in this situation. You will instinctively know what to say and what not to say. Indicate if you believe they would be interested in hearing your deceased loved one's old stories, memories, or quotes. There will inevitably be topics that you should not discuss, so keep your yap shut. Continue conversing and avoid letting your recollections flood back like a waterfall.

My funeral address for Bob was not straightforward. And I am cognizant of anyone in my position. However, we must learn to control our emotions, communicate openly, express our sentiments to the deceased friend, and share our suffering with our families.

Funerals are likely the last thing anyone wishes to do, but we must still attend them because we care about our friend or loved one. Nobody attended Bob Woolf's funeral to hear Larry King speak. We all went there to bid Bob farewell and because we owed him one.

I will now give you my portion. If you ever find yourself in my position and must speak at a funeral, just keep in mind that no one is there to hear you. They came to convey their sorrow over the loss of a family member. to ruminate on the life of the deceased. Please convey your regret and condolences to the bereaved. Occasionally, a little humor can help to enliven a gloomy situation. Always remember that speaking less is preferable.

DISCUSS WITH STARS

Speaking with renowned individuals is a daunting undertaking for many individuals. Especially when they are "passive" because of his (or her) notoriety.

You will be extremely confused if you do not prepare mentally. Top musicians, actors, and athletes... There are times when you are at a loss for words when speaking to them because you lack sufficient knowledge or have never worked in their profession. Being inherently sensitive, communicating with stars requires extreme tact. They will certainly cringe if you claim to have adored them since childhood. Even if you do not intend it, they presume you are referring to their age. Your statement, "In the past, my father took me to watch him kick" (and now he no longer does?!), will hurt the athletes' feelings.

If you said, "I always envisioned myself as a famous singer (or movie actor, or football player)," the star's popularity would be significantly diminished. You are communicating. They will believe you when you say that anyone can complete the task.

For my television programs, I conduct a large number of interviews with well-known individuals from all aspects of life. You can be certain that stars enjoy cordial conversation as much as I do with you. I do not give the impression that I am speaking to a celebrity when I speak to them. You will fail if you allow their stellar reputation to dictate your actions. They are human like us. In addition, children share our emotions and have similar preferences for other things. I was able to hold a casual conversation with them.

When viewed from this perspective, conversing with a notable individual becomes an enthralling opportunity. They are exceptional individuals with novel concepts.

Chapter 14: Don't Only Discuss Yourself

You will likely discuss yourself in conversation. However, avoid speaking exclusively of yourself. Learn more about the other person by addressing them directly: "How about you, Mary? "Do you work anywhere?"

Feelings, SHARE

In retrospect, the individuals with whom we appreciate conversing the most are frequently those who are most similar to us. They care about our opinions and feelings. You want people to respond to the news of your new position with "Wow, that's incredible!" rather than "Oh, really?" or "Is that so?"

Oprah Winfrey, a well-known television spokesperson for many Americans, has always demonstrated genuine concern for her visitors' emotional state. Clearly, Oprah is always interested in hearing what others have to say. This is what connects her to everyone. Oprah is the successful ambassador that we all venerate due to one simple strategy.

All effective spokespersons possess this characteristic. They are known by the term commiserators. If you confide in them that you have a brain tumor or are simply timid, they will immediately sympathize with you and may even be anxious to assist you. Sonya Friedman, who hosts CNN's weekend program "Sony Live," is an excellent example. Dick Cavett is an additional persuasive spokesperson. A person who is extremely sensitive and is always concerned with the stories, thoughts, and emotions of their visitors. Cavett does not need to look elsewhere for bizarre concepts because he is already aware that this lends the show "character."

DISPLAY YOUR HORRIFIC

Conversations are enhanced by the presence of humor. Sometimes it's crucial to employ levity. When delivering a speech, one of my governing principles is to "never speak too long or too seriously."

However, forced humor does not work, just as it does not work in real life. The greatest comedians are aware of this and do not attempt to elicit laughter from the audience. I'll give you an illustration. Robert Hope Bob never intentionally attempted to be humorous. He is never rigid and monotonous, constantly cracking quips at parties and on stage, in the media, and during variety programs. He is also a prosperous businessman. He is always involved in charitable endeavors and inquisitive about current events. As a result, Bob's sense of humor is extremely diverse and robust.

Al Pacino is another person with a strong inherent sense of humor. Offstage, he is a humorous character, despite being one of the most talented stage actors in the United States. A calm New Yorker brushes off life's many dangers.

Al Pacino, Walter Cronkite, soccer legend Pele, myself, and a few others were conversing in the Beverly Wilshire hotel lobby in January 1994, just hours after a major earthquake. We were all, including some of us, stunned. Pacino is the only individual to shrug and respond, "I'm from New York, I thought it was a bomb!" Certainly, Pacino did not intend to ridicule him; he simply said "tree" out of habit. However, we all had to chuckle. The tension was relieved by Pacino's remarks.

Another character with a distinct sense of humor. George Burns fits the description. He rarely had anything to say besides quips, and humor came to him as naturally as his own existence. At a celebration, everyone discusses their health, and each individual has unique concerns. George was asked about his general opinion of physicians. George retorted, "I consume two glasses of wine at noon and two more at night." "Every day, I smoke ten cigars." I appreciate conversing with young ladies. People ask my nearly 100-year-old self what my physician says about this." – The last time I saw my doctor was ten years ago, George calmly added after halting to survey the table.

Indeed, George Burns is George Burns! People chuckle at the mere mention of his daily activities. These facts are common knowledge, but George's words make them seem intriguing. George's peculiar tone and delivery of "nothing" may be to blame.

Don Rickles is an individual who relishes telling jokes in both public and private settings. Undesirable behaviors and aspects of life are all rendered humorous by Rickles' sense of humor. Why can he amuse everyone but neither you nor I? Because of Rickles, humor is ingrained in our nature. He is neither pretentious nor unduly funny. This should be remembered.

Choose the appropriate time to be humorous. Never interrupt someone in order to tell a jest or an amusing story.

Every persuasive speaker has their own distinct approach. Let's examine and evaluate the four eccentricities of the four most successful attorneys in the United States during the second half of the 20th century.

Edward Bennett Williams communicates extremely slowly and softly. These considerate and perceptive remarks are persuasive in court. Without your knowledge, they gradually take over your consciousness and subjugate you. This strategy yielded significant success for Edward.

Percy Foreman, another well-known attorney, always has something persuasive to say, whether he is addressing a jury or a lunch guest. He chose to use emotive language and captivated his audience from beginning to end with a fluent, comprehensible, and captivating delivery. Because this is Percy's method, he simplifies the situation.

Williams Kunstler is an attorney with a commanding, resolute presence. A person who is prone to anger. Every time Williams entered the courtroom, the atmosphere became hostile and animated. Williams and his colleagues are successful despite their styles being the complete opposite of those of Edward and Percy.

Louis Nizer prefers to say that he creates prospective dramatic situations by constructing a chain of events. If Kunstler draws you in with intensity and Nizer persuades you with precision and logic, Edward and Percy appeal to your emotions.

Even though you are not the attorneys in the courtroom, there is still much you can learn from them. Finding and perfecting your own speaking approach is essential. Otherwise, people will not be impressed after speaking with you, and you will be incredibly dull.

I am regularly asked, "What is Larry King's personal style?" However, describing one's own style is significantly more challenging than describing another's. I believe that my speech pattern resembles Cavett's, a style that combines and rotates without expressing emotion. Sometimes fierce, sometimes gentle, sometimes hesitant, sometimes resolute... I improvise in response to a variety of circumstances and feelings. Please share your thoughts regarding Larry King's presentation style if you see me on CNN.

One final point: only appropriate silence

I recall vividly a pivotal moment in "The Honeymooners," a classic comedy. Audrey Meadows and my friend Jackie Gleason both play Ralph (as Alice) in this play. Ralph stared straight ahead and placed his finger in the center of Alice's face as she vacillated between unintentionally and intentionally revealing his plans. "Alice, you are such a talkative person!" he exclaimed.

Even if you have an excellent speaking voice, there are times when it is best to be mute. You must master self-control in all social situations. Avoid using abusive language and pay attention to what your senses are telling you: silence is not preferable. Because occasionally, silence speaks volumes. Occasionally, silence is all that is required for someone to comprehend what you mean.

Chapter 15: Communication Dissection Dilemma

Attempts to Resolve the Conflict That Failed

When individuals perceive tension in a relationship that was not previously present, they attempt to resolve it by "talking about it." Unfortunately, when we discuss it, we frequently say and do inappropriate things. Period. We just do. Why? Because we acquired our communicative skills and behaviors from external influences. We never embraced our true and authentic selves and communicated our relationship desires and needs. We attempt to alleviate tension in an effort to make the relationship more tolerable, but we fail and sometimes make matters worse.

We may attempt one or more of the following five methods to resolve relationship tensions through communication. Although the list that follows is not exhaustive, I have highlighted the most common strategies that you are likely familiar with. None of these are effective, and they frequently increase relationship tension. They consist of passive antagonism, comedy/sarcasm, explosive outbursts, ignoring the situation, and staging an intervention. Let's examine each in depth.

Passive aggression is a deliberate and disguised method of expressing repressed wrath. It consists of a variety of behaviors intended to exact revenge on another individual without acknowledging the underlying fury. It is clearly unresolved hostility. It can also be cyclical. Everyone knows someone who does this. We may even perform this action. It does not function, but many of us rely on it nonetheless.

You may resort to passive aggression in an attempt to defuse a tense situation because you believe that people will respond in the way you desire to hostile acts and words. The belief is that the other individual will change if they experience sufficient pain. You may even presume that the recipient will eventually decipher your encoded messages because "who wouldn't decipher the messages?" According to Pastor Rick Warren, author of Purpose Driven Life and pastor of Saddleback Church, however, people do not change when they see the light; they change when they experience the heat. I concur with his viewpoint. This means that individuals do not change as a result of acquiring new information or becoming aware of certain truths. People do not abandon hazardous behavior because they are apprehended, shot, "hit rock bottom," or incarcerated. People change when they perceive that they have no other option. When people ultimately confront themselves and live with the consequences of what they have done, who they have become, and who they are in that moment, and when they can no longer run or hide from that reflection, only then will they be able to change. Despite this fact, we erroneously believe that another individual will "pick up on a subliminal message." That is simply not how humans are constructed.

For example, let's contemplate drug addiction. A close friend has smoked marijuana their entire existence without incident. Right? After years of marijuana use, their behavior gradually changes. They do not appear when you arrange to meet for happy hour. They begin to call in ill for work. They also appear to disappear for days at a time. As an acquaintance, you suspect that there is more going on than marijuana use, but you cannot be certain. When you go to visit, you encounter some shady and suspicious individuals who are referred to as "new friends." A crack pipe and needles are observed on the coffee table. You dash out of the home in complete disbelief. But before you do, you say, "I know you smoked marijuana, but I thought you were intelligent enough to avoid harder drugs!" To add insult to injury, you later visit the friend's residence to drop off narcotics anonymous pamphlets.

The problem rests therein. What is its meaning? What should your acquaintance take away from these actions? Moreover, what are they expected to do after being subjected to judgment, humiliation, and general cruelty?

Nothing will work if you do not communicate your authentic self. In this situation, you want to convey your friend that it is heartbreaking to observe their physical decline due to drug use. You would like to inform them that you avoid spending time with their children because you do not wish to explain addiction. You want to inform them that you are upset that you have lost a best friend and are unsure if you will ever see them again. You want to tell them that this addiction has also altered your existence. But instead, you just leave pamphlets in a letterbox.

The use of comedy or sarcasm verbally expresses hostility, but in socially acceptable, indirect ways. There is always an element of truth in comedic quips; this is what makes them amusing and occasionally painful. People have used humor to hide their suffering for centuries. Consider Kevin Hart's groundbreaking comedy special Laugh at My Pain and Chris Rock's classic comedy tour Bring the Pain. In each of these, they use humor to discuss real-life problems, often forbidden subjects that are not discussed, such as drug addiction and imprisonment, which is humorous because we have all experienced the deafening silence that these topics can bring to a friendship or a family. Humor is an essential tool for making stories more memorable, characters more engaging, and causes more accessible.

On the other hand, people can use comedy to express their frustration in a subtle and socially acceptable manner. We frequently use humor to defuse tension because we believe it's best to deliver a negative message while everyone is chuckling and enjoying themselves. We mistakenly believe that if someone is laughing, they are more receptive to what is being said and will "take the hint."

Let's revisit the example of substance addiction. After the failure of passive antagonism, you believe comedic outbursts may succeed. Your friend was able to gather enough people to attend your backyard barbecue. While music plays and people dance in the yard, a few of you are dining and conversing at the table. The topic of discussion shifts to the recent break-ins in the area. Several friends discuss the additional precautions they are taking to prevent burglaries, while others joke about alarm systems and the notion of getting a dog for protection. Then you say, "You don't need alarms or dogs if your closest friend will steal $20 from your dining room table. The group experiences an awkward pause, which is soon followed by hysterical laughter and high-fives. Clearly distressed, your acquaintance walks away in disgrace. The others are unaware that your closest friend stole money from you in order to purchase drugs.

You shake your head in disbelief instead of chasing after your friend to offer comfort or at least attempt to speak about it. You believed they might have $20 on them to repay you and apologize. However, because they left, you believe they are angry because you "told everybody" about what they did. However, you will never know because you never discuss it.

Explosive outbursts are actions and/or responses that are disproportionate to the situation (e.g., impulsive shouting, shrieking, or excessive reprimanding in response to relatively insignificant events). There are both physical and verbal outbursts. Everyone experiences anger at moments. In a split second, anger can range from mild irritation to full-blown fury. Frequently, we attempt to lock up or control our emotions until we can no longer do so. Then, we resort to verbal explosions because it feels good to let everything out. To yell and scream at someone or to leap on them and fight relieves tension. It grants you control over your actions, and no one can stop you. All that matters is that you were able to clearly communicate your point to everyone. Unfortunately, outbursts appear to come out of nowhere, and the intended target or innocent bystanders are frequently left perplexed. Frequently, they wonder, "Where did that come from?" or "What caused that?"

Using the analogy of drug addiction, we can see that outbursts occur but are not beneficial. In this instance, your acquaintance has further descended into addiction and has been evicted from their home. They are currently residing in destitute shelters or on the couches of relatives who feel pity for them. A friend calls and asks if you are available to fetch them up. They're stuck on the opposite side of the metropolis. They explain that some men assaulted them and seized their vehicle. You scream into the phone, "You deserve everything you receive!" You destroyed your existence. Drugs are detrimental to you, your family, and the majority of your acquaintances. I have no idea why you called me. I will not assist you any longer. I'm tired of cleaning up after your errors. You brought this upon yourself. Nobody made you use narcotics. Nobody forced a pipe or a syringe into your mouth or arm. I no longer know who you are. I am exhausted by this!" You shut up the phone without waiting for a response in order to emphasize your point.

Unfortunately, the outburst has only caused additional damage. The friend called you because they believed you were their only remaining friend. They are aware that narcotics have destroyed their lives. Your acquaintance wishes they had never begun any of it. But they cannot cease now because they are a drug addict and have no idea how to quit. Your outburst was motivated by anger because you care about your friend and cannot bear to see them lose control. You hope that perhaps hearing "the truth" will finally set them straight. You are both left with a sense of loss and sorrow, as well as lingering thoughts about how to restore the friendship. However, you will never know because you never discuss it.

4. Ignoring (acting as if nothing occurred) is impossible, although many attempt it. Subconsciously, we are aware of the problem even if we are not consciously aware of it or if we do nothing about it. The fact that we choose to disregard it allows unresolved emotions to manifest in other aspects of the relationship. The act of ignoring can manifest itself in various ways: we can cease all communication ("I will never call them again"), we can walk away when the subject is brought up ("I left something in my car"), or we can claim complete ignorance of the subject ("No, I didn't know that"). Although not an exhaustive list, these are the most popular options most individuals select.

Regarding drug addiction, it is regrettably acceptable in today's society to disregard the issue. For instance, while walking to the local coffee shop one day, you see your drug addict acquaintance sitting on the corner. You choose to use your phone instead of making eye contact. You hope your friend doesn't notice you. However, you are not the only one ignoring them now. At the request of their ex-partner, the coach had security escort them off the field when they attempted to attend their son's baseball game. Even their mother disregards the issue. When she was with her family, someone inquired about her children's health. She cut the query off and excused herself to use the restroom. It is sometimes easier to ignore the individual and the issue than to communicate directly about them.

Intervention is frequently associated with addiction in order to encourage individuals to seek treatment. However, we can use interventions to address a variety of destructive behaviors (such as infidelity and neglecting responsibilities) that negatively impact individuals and those around them. Typically, intervention is a last resort, the last chance individuals have to make a change.

An intervention includes demands and a unified front. The purpose is to demonstrate that family and friends continue to adore and care for the individual. But it can only function if everyone is given the chance to express their sincere feelings about how the situation has affected their lives. An intervention is not about reaching a consensus or getting the facts straight; rather, it is about providing a space and the opportunity to express feelings and emotions without passing judgment. However, it is crucial to recognize that even though those who participate in the intervention have high hopes for a positive outcome (the person will enter rehab), they must be willing to accept that the outcome may be unpredictable and may be very different from their expectations.

If we consider our drug addiction story as a final example of intervention, we realize that not everyone is receptive to the offered assistance or the affection shown by family and friends during the process. In this situation, you determine to attempt to save your friend's life. You've heard that they served time in prison and are currently destitute. All of their relatives have left because your friend stole from them or lied to them. Their family fears they can no longer assist. You invite your friend's ex-partner, mother, and several cousins to participate in the intervention. Everyone agrees to participate, but only after relating their horrific experiences with this individual.

Finally, the day of the intervention arrives. You have a unified front, and you all believe this strategy may succeed. Your acquaintance has arrived. Everyone feels similarly about how substance use has affected their lives. The loss of safety whenever they appear... the sadness of not having a child, cousin, or friend in their life anymore ... The humiliation of seeing them begging on the streets. You want this individual to seek aid.

Unfortunately, your friend thinks they have hurt too many people, caused too much damage, and will never get their life back on track. Your friend stands up and offers a heartfelt apology, "I am sorry for all the pain I have caused each of you." They then leave the room in a commotion. Everyone is shocked. You wonder, "What do we do now?" No one has an answer for what is next. It's too painful to talk about, so you never discuss it again.

Forging A Way Forward

All of the aforementioned strategies are typical methods for attempting to defuse relationship tension. Because we believe we have no control, we attempt to gain control by discussing the issue directly. However, this only adds additional stress and strain to the relationship's existing tension. It causes fury denial, leaves actions open to interpretation, and creates an emotional roller coaster for all parties involved.

We can all agree that we do the majority of these things because we urgently want to restore the relationship to its pre-incident state, but do not know how. That's not to say we can't. It merely indicates that we must establish a new norm, new boundaries, and new expectations for the relationship. New and improved relationships are feasible!

To transition to the new relationship, you must reconnect and reestablish the connection by discussing the tension. The required labor will not be accomplished overnight. The road to a new relationship may be arduous and convoluted. The journey will be unique for each individual and relationship. This work will necessitate that each individual assume responsibility for their role and actions within the relationship. No longer can you wait to see what will transpire. Now is the moment for action!

You must be deliberate and purposeful regarding your intentions, actions, and words. Others might not be receptive to your actions or words. You may discover that the other person is not interested in a romantic relationship. Perhaps the other party does not wish to communicate. That's alright. You will need to adopt a new mentality in order to achieve your objective of understanding communication and becoming a more effective communicator. Ultimately, if you alter your speech and mentality, you can alter your life and relationships. It matters what you say, how you say it, and when you say it.

Your words are extremely potent. The tongue holds the power of life and death. Death transcends the tangible. Psychological and emotional death ("I am meaningless. They only act as if they like me. I am defective merchandise") can originate from the tongue, even when self-directed.

Words matter. YOUR opinions have value! Understanding communication is important because true communication can only occur when there is mutual understanding. As a result, we will spend the next several chapters discussing interpersonal communication and how it has a significant impact on life and relationships, as well as providing you with tools and techniques to restore your relationships.

Are you prepared to resolve the strained relationships? Let's get moving.

Conclusion

Here are several essential principles and takeaways regarding effective communication:

Good communication skills are necessary for establishing and maintaining relationships, effectively solving problems, resolving conflicts, and attaining one's objectives.

Listening attentively is an essential communication skill that involves paying close attention to what another person is saying and demonstrating engagement in the conversation.

Asking open-ended inquiries can be useful for fostering discussion and dialogue, getting to know someone better, gathering more information, and establishing rapport.

Handling challenging or delicate topics requires cautious communication skills, a respectful approach, and a focus on finding common ground and solutions.

Staying calm and in control during challenging conversations requires self-awareness, the establishment of clear boundaries, and the application of effective communication skills.

Effective communication at work requires active listening, the use of plain and concise language, a professional tone, consideration of the audience, respect, and effective written communication.

Effective communication in social situations requires active listening, the use of open-ended questions, respect, the use of nonverbal cues, consideration for others, and excellent manners.

Effective communication with family and friends requires being open and honest, practicing active listening, employing "I" statements, demonstrating empathy, respecting boundaries, and seeking assistance when necessary.

Improving one's communication abilities is always a wise course of action. Effective communication is necessary for establishing and maintaining relationships, solving problems efficiently, and attaining one's objectives.

You can continue to enhance your communication abilities and become a more effective communicator by exercising these skills and seeking feedback.